THE
LAST WILL
AND
TESTAMENT
OF SMALL
BUSINESS

DAN PHILLIPS

ISBN: 1466460458
ISBN 13: 9781466460454

CONTENTS

FOREWORD IX

CHAPTER 1:
Last Will and Testament of the Small Business 1

CHAPTER 2: 5
Health-Care Power of Attorney

CHAPTER 3: 9
How did we Get in this Mess

CHAPTER 4: 27
Early Viruses that got into Government

CHAPTER 5: 45
First Diagnoses of Disease and Why Sba was Started

CHAPTER 6: 65
No one is Spending Money

CHAPTER 7: 77
The Invasion and takeover of the Big Box and Chain Stores

CHAPTER 8: 119
The Truth

CHAPTER 9: 129
The Future of Small Business

CHAPTER 10: 139
We Bequeath the Following

CHAPTER 11: 157
How to Correct the Course

Acknowledgments

Some of our founders knew what was coming.

'I predict future happiness for Americans if they can prevent the government from wasting the labors of the people under the pretense of taking care of them."

Thomas Jefferson

'History records that the money changers have used every form of abuse, intrigue, deceit, and violent means possible to maintain their control over governments by controlling the money and its issuance."

James Madison

THIS IS WHAT HE MAY HAVE KNOWN COULD HAPPEN!

$16,000,000,000,000.00 had been secretly given out to US banks and corporations and foreign banks everywhere from France to Scotland. From the period between December 2007 and June 2010, the Federal Reserve had secretly bailed out many of the world's banks, corporations, and governments.

Reserve had secretly bailed out many of the world's banks, corporations, and governments.

The list of institutions that received the most money from the Federal Reserve can be found on page 131 of the GAO Audit and are as follows.

Citigroup: $2.5 trillion ($2,500,000,000,000)
Morgan Stanley: $2.04 trillion ($2,040,000,000,000)
Merrill Lynch: $1.949 trillion ($1,949,000,000,000)
Bank of America: $1.344 trillion ($1,344,000,000,000)
Barclays PLC (United Kingdom): $868 billion
($868,000,000,000)
Bear Sterns: $853 billion ($853,000,000,000)
Goldman Sachs: $814 billion ($814,000,000,000)
Royal Bank of Scotland (UK): $541 billion
($541,000,000,000)
JP Morgan Chase: $391 billion ($391,000,000,000)
Deutsche Bank (Germany): $354 billion
($354,000,000,000)
UBS (Switzerland): $287 billion ($287,000,000,000)
Credit Suisse (Switzerland): $262 billion
($262,000,000,000)
Lehman Brothers: $183 billion ($183,000,000,000)
Bank of Scotland (United Kingdom): $181 billion
($181,000,000,000)
BNP Paribas (France): $175 billion
($175,000,000,000)
And many more including banks in Belgium of all
places.

PRIOR TO THIS HAPPENING THE FOLLOWING WAS GOING ON.

While we have been all caught up with the internet, technology and going to soccer practice we have not been paying attention to some very key things happening.

Take the time to look at how many mergers and acquisitions have gone on while we were looking elsewhere.

Look especially at the industries that they have happened in. If you think back about this you will remember how whenever competition to any of these larger companies came into the picture they were acquired for the purpose of maintaining control or to hide the true balance sheet from Wall Street and Stockholders.

- *Transportation (Airlines, trucking, car companies etc.)*
- *Communications (Cell Phones,)*
- *Media (Cable)*
- *Grocers*
- *Computers*
- *Chains Stores*
- *Financial(Banks)*
- *Petroleum*
- *Energy*
- *Insurance Companies*

Also look at the growth of all the governments from national down to local.

If you take the time to count how many of these businesses that we have grown to depend on in our everyday lives you will begin to see the impending dilemma.

Add up your Monthly expenses and then see what options you have to lower them by changing to the competitor.

This might begin to enlighten you of how quickly we have become dependent on Monopolies.

FOREWORD

(We) throughout the book is intended to mean Small Business.

There are many stories about the death or impending death of small businesses.

Now that we have progressed to Stage 3 of our illness we felt it wise at this time to do a Will.

Just like any responsible party should do for their family, we felt it was only prudent to be prepared to leave the proper legacy for current small businesses and the ones to come.

We have left a Health-Care Power of Attorney as well.

We would like to start by saying that it has been an honor to be a small business in America and to be the driving force behind the economy since the birth of this nation.

If you study history, you will find that small businesses have generated more jobs, generated more wealth, paid more taxes, developed more patents and started and maintained the Countries economic engine from the very start.

We have always been Americans who have turned ideas into jobs.

**Small Business believes in Capitalism we helped started it.**

While we are still of sound mind we would like to pass on the things that we have experienced that have made it more difficult to start, and grow a small business during the last twenty years and especially during the current economic times.

Since our forefathers fought and died for our freedom, we have had the right to start and run a business. As we proceed through our Will, we will share with you the highs and lows of our struggle.

This isn't about the Tea Party, Coffee Party, Republican, Democratic, Independent, Libertarian Parties or any current or prior Presidents. This is about saving the American economy instead of standing on the sidelines and watching it be destroyed or pointing fingers.

For those of you who get your feelings hurt easy or don't like old people (small businesses) expressing their opinions, you may want to take your meds early and often, because a lot of toes will be stepped on.

We add the caveat that there are exceptions to the rule in all of the groups mentioned. To those exceptions, we sincerely apologize and appreciate you. You know who you are and will know when these comments are not meant for you.

One of our early Presidents Andrew Jackson put things in perspective very well.

Even when the General was dying he said *that "all would be well" if Americans stayed away from Monopolies.*

You will find how much of a visionary he and others were as you progress through this book.

This book is intended to show how important small business has been to this country in the past. It is also going to show why we are sick and who has caused our illness.

It will through its ideas and common sense show how it can and will lead us out of this economic ditch that our government has allowed.

CHAPTER 1

LAST WILL AND TESTAMENT OF THE SMALL BUSINESS

We, Small Business of America, do hereby make, publish, and declare this to be our Last Will and Testament, and we hereby revoke all Wills and codicils heretofore made by us.

ARTICLE I

We direct that if funeral expenses are needed, including the cost of a suitable grave markers (*possibly a gone-out-of-business sign, or you could use some of those empty billboards*), the cost of administering our estates and all debts allowable as claims be paid by the all groups mentioned in this book and especially the government that refused to see the obvious signs that we were the reason the economy has always grown and they were too greedy or stupid to recognize that.

ARTICLE II

We direct that all estate, inheritance, succession, legacy and any other taxes be waived and paid to worthy causes of our choice (*humane society, hospice, etc.*). Any compensation for the executors, *our brother and sister small businesses, should be in the form of low or no interest loans without all the red tape to get them, a level playing field for competition, and a government that gets out of the way.*

ARTICLE III

What we are willing to bequeath will be outlined later in our Will. (We hope you enjoy that part.)

ARTICLE IV

We, Small Business of America, the testators, sign our name to this instrument this 17th day of June, 2011, and being first duly sworn, do hereby declare to the under-signed authority that we sign and execute this instrument as our Last Will and Testament, that we sign it reluctantly, that we execute it as a forced act for the purposes therein expressed, and that we are at least 235 years of age or older and under major pressure and restraints.

SMALL BUSINESSES OF AMERICA

We, the *government, Wall Street, lobbyists, media, drug companies, insurance industry, big-box stores, and chain stores, the witnesses*, sign our names to this instrument, first admitting our screw-ups and greed, and do hereby declare to the undersigned authority that the testators. Small businesses signs and executes this as their Last Will and Testament, and signs it screaming, spitting, kicking, and yelling. Each of us, in the presence and hearing of the testators, hereby signs this Will as witnesses to the testator's signing, and that to the best of our knowledge, the testators are at least 235 years old, of sound mind, have been around long before us, and know that we have screwed over them for close to that long and will continue to do so unless stopped.

Name:	**Address:**
Government	Every State, City, County and Town, USA
Wall Street	Wall Street
Lobbyist	Any Rock You Look Under
Media	Every Home
Big-Box Stores and Chains	Every Corner Everywhere

United States of America
All States and Counties

Subscribed and sworn before me by Small Business of America, the testators, and subscribed and sworn before me by <u>witnesses above,</u> this 17th day of June 2011.

_____
                              Attorney General USA
My Commission Expires: _____

CHAPTER 2

HEALTH-CARE POWER OF ATTORNEY

Every State, USA—All Counties

In this document, we designate to our health-care agent broad powers to make health-care decisions for us, including the power to consent to your doctor (*please spend longer than the 7 minutes with us when we are in your office*) not giving you the treatment necessary to keep you alive. This power relates only to those health-care decisions for which you are unable to give informed consent. (It is difficult to give them anything with the obstacles listed below.)

1. <u>Designation of Health-Care Agent</u>

We, Small Business of America, hereby appoint:
Names: *The American People with the exceptions of lawyers, lobbyists, bankers, big-box stores or*

chains, insurance companies, media outlets, and drug companies.
Address: USA
Telephone No: ***Dial 911 if any of the above-mentioned comes into room.***

2. General Statement of Authority Granted

We grant authority to the remaining small businesses and the American people to decide our long-term fate.

We authorize you to decide if the parties mentioned above and below are to be the ones to lead us into the future.

We authorize and consent for you to decide if they will be allowed to withhold any and all measures needed for our long-term survival. Be very careful if the only groups hiring are the few mentioned they will own your soul.

We request that you review the information that has been included before you make decision.

You had better really think about the research needed to decide if you really need to stop life sustaining measures. The decision made prematurely may cost you your freedom.

3. Special Provisions and Limitations

We ask that before you watch us die, try whatever means necessary to provide life-sustaining measures.

- You may be saving the economy and your retirement.

- If this means driving fifteen minutes further to shop local, do it.
- If this means paying a dollar or 10 percent more, do it.
- If this means driving past the fast food chains and eat at local restaurants they would appreciate the business.
- If this means searching the Internet or the Yellow Pages past the obvious names to do business with us, do it.
- If you have to leave a message on a machine rather than press 8 different numbers before you speak to someone in India, we are out working and we will call you back.

We retain the right to ignore this document and survive with the help of the people who understand what small business has done for America. We have done it from the beginning, and we will do it again. We want to give everyone the opportunity to help pull the economy out of the ditch sooner.

4. Signature of Principle

By signing here, we indicate that we are mentally alert and competent, fully informed as to the contents of this document, and understand the full import of this grant of power to my health-care agents.

_____
Small Business of America
Date:_____

5. Signature of Witnesses

We hereby state that the principal, Small Business of America, being of sound mind, signed the foregoing health-care power of attorney in our presence.

_____

Witness: Date
All Americans

Witness:
Entrepreneurs of the Future

_____

Date

CHAPTER 3

HOW DID WE GET
INTO THIS MESS?

The definition for Testament is as follows: *Testament* - strong evidence for something.

This will be our supporting evidence for how we will divide or estate.

Over the last twenty years, small businesses with fewer than one hundred employees have logged close _**to twenty-six billion days (26,000,000,000) of on-the-job training**_. We feel that experience qualifies us to make the following observations and suggestions.

Let's cut to the chase quickly.

Some of these points are obvious, but humor us as we are old and for the first part of this treat us like we are old and ill and you want us to remember you as being respectful.

The current economic health issues in the United States are:

- Our economy seems to have 1 foot in the grave and the other on a banana peel.
- Media reports say no companies are hiring.
- As a result unemployment is growing. Now unemployment is being said to be 34% in El Centro California and 29.4% in Yuma Arizona.
- Banks are not lending and are canceling credit lines.
- Large companies are laying off, even the companies the government took over because no one is buying.
- Debt is going up because the unemployed don't pay taxes and government is either clueless or is on a different mission other than putting people back to work. They have now extended unemployment where people can stay on it for over 2 years.

All the while the Government is standing around pointing fingers and getting ready to run for reelection on all fronts and spending more money on campaigns than the GDP of a lot of countries.

- Also the government keeps coming up with these jobs plans (stimulus) that have done nothing for the employment numbers and increasing our debt.
- During this time we are being fed more false information from the Media with the purpose of trying to keep us from really knowing what the truth is.
- Because "We can't Handle the Truth" *(line from the Movie Officer and Gentleman)
- Probably the only people making money are the people on Wall Street manipulating the market up and down.

THAT ABOUT SUMS IT UP!

SOME OVERLOOKED SYMPTOMS OF OUR ILLNESS.

As we continue through our Testament, we are sure you think the small business ("old folks") have had a seizure and lost it. Bear with us. We have been through a lot, and we assure you that you will see the reasoning along the way. We may be old and slow, but with age comes wisdom.

Who would like to stand up, raise their hand, and take responsibility for the economic mess we are in?

We will.

You should too.

Let's be honest. To start to heal and correct the course of the country, we have to accept the responsibility.

Most of us don't vote and have no idea who is on the ballot and what they stand for If you think through that logic for a second you realize that a large number of people are getting into all offices that you have no idea what they stand for or what decisions they will make.

There are surveys that election consultants and lobbyist use to exploit every election at every level. All experienced incumbents know a dirty little truth: *most House elections are over six months to a year before they are held.* Experienced members of the press know the same thing, but they dare not report it.

Conflict sells newspapers and gets people to watch TV. That, in turn, sells cars, beer, and deodorant. If there isn't any real conflict in congressional races, false conflict will do just as well, as long as the public hasn't caught on. Those are bold charges. They can be proved.

(**John C. Armor)

Keep something else in mind. It looks like in 2012; the candidate for president will spend a billion dollars to get elected. Not one penny of that will do a thing for the economy

Thank you, media and lobbyists.

This is the vicious cycle we have gotten in. When you really look at what is going on, Washington is about reelection from all side and all parties.

The sad truth is that once most candidates get into office very few people ever know how they vote on any of the issues brought before them.

A lot of people are hurting and need to realize that they are responsible for most of it themselves.

There is an old saying that states, "If you are in a ditch, the way to get out of it is to stop digging." The current state of the economy is a very deep ditch, and the government is using the largest machine made to continue digging.

Why are a lot of the decision makers in national, state and local governments ignoring the fact that small business has always been the greatest job generator? It could be it is because entrepreneurs are free independent thinkers and are harder to control. The Government would say that they are doing their part by funding the SBA. At the same time they are throwing a Trillion dollars at failed stimulus plans.

We do know that we started and generated more jobs than all the major companies put together.

For years, we have believed that our government and the elected officials have decided to make permanent jobs and nest eggs for themselves in Washington and other state capitols.

Congress for Life

The Problem of Careerism in Congress and a Case for Term Limits

By John Armor

"For the first 125 years of American history under its new Constitution, we were governed by citizen representatives in Congress and in the White House. Tradition, not legal requirements, maintained this condition.

Presidents followed the example of George Washington, who served two terms as president and then went home, not because he was forced to but because he believed in "rotation in office." That meant elected leaders would not always remain in office, but would in turn be the governed, rather than the rulers.

A similar, less noticed change was occurring in Congress at the same time. The tradition there was that members would serve perhaps two terms in the House, one or maybe two in the Senate, and then return to their homes to live under the laws they had written.

For our first 125 years, about 35 percent of the members of the House retired before every election. They were not usually faced with potential defeat if they chose to run again. These were "voluntary quits", members who went home because they believed that was good for them and good for the nation.

Average turnover in the House for the entire first century of our government was 43 percent in every election. There were a few convictions or expulsions then, as now and there were deaths.

This, in turn, draws more and stronger challengers into the races. The goal of gerrymandering, whether done by Republicans or Democrats, is to make seats stronger for the more influential incumbents, meaning those with most seniority and clout. So, long-term incumbents get districts with higher proportions of voters in their party. That makes them safer in the general election. But in redistricting years only, it makes them more vulnerable in party primaries.

Until 1900, there were only two years in which the voluntary quit rate was below 15 percent (1808 and 1870). Since 1902, there has only been one year in which the voluntary quit rate rose above 15 percent (1912). The effect has been most pronounced in the 27 elections beginning in 1938. In all but five of those, the voluntary quit rate has been less than 10 percent. (The exceptions are 1952, and 1972–78.). This one major change, declining voluntary quits, is the key to the exceptionally low turnover rates in the House in the 20th century.

The key points here are the reasons for the turnover in congressional positions in the early years of our country were voluntary, death or expulsion. This could only mean that Congressman or Senators had to go home and make a living (more than likely owning or working for a small business) or they tried to make it off the American people's money and got caught with their hand in the cookie jar.

Our leaders in DC running the show have put themselves in a financial position so that they have nothing to worry about.

It has become very obvious that they don't care about the small business man or the American people.

Small business had to go out every day, build our businesses, hire new workers, pay taxes, and carry the economy on our backs.

That doesn't speak for the fact that during that time as a small business, we had to risk everything. When we say risk everything we mean leveraging our homes and all of our collateral.

The lifestyles that Congress carries on while in DC are the type of thing that we cannot believe. It has become common place that our money being wasted is old news and not worth talking about or being printed in the media."

This is a table that shows different members in Congress and their net worth from 2004-2009. We will be fair and say that none of this had anything to do with their position in Congress.

They are all very wise businesspeople who are smarter than the rest of the working American Public who have lost money or are drawing out of their savings at an alarming rate.

It could probably be shown by facts and figures that there is no distinctly American criminal class except Congress. -Mark Twain

"The List" of the Elite 80: Skyrocketing Net Worth

41 Democrats	Avg '04	Avg '08	Growth '04-'08	% Chg.	2009 Net Worth	
Gutierrez, Luis V (D-Ill)	$47,503	$1,790,508	$1,743,005	3,669	>100% Gain	$2,358,005
Scott, David (D-Ga)	$107,262	$3,008,001	$2,900,739	2,704	>100% Gain	$3,758,001
Sanchez, Loretta (D-Calif)	$196,505	$2,547,501	$2,350,996	1,196	>100% Gain	$2,474,001
Sanchez, Linda (D-Calif)	-$32,500	$342,500	$375,000	1,154	>100% Gain	$751,010
Herseth Sandlin, Stephanie (D-SD)	-$112,000	$1,152,510	$1,264,510	1,129	>100% Gain	$1,332,853
Obama, Barack	$300,002	$3,670,505	$3,370,503	1,124	>100% Gain	$4,960,505
Feingold, Russ (D-Wis)	$8,000	$83,501	$75,501	944	>100% Gain	$83,001

Hinchey, Maurice (D-NY)	$74,002	$727,509	$653,507	883	>100% Gain	$743,508
Eshoo, Anna (D-Calif)	-$385,996	$1,508,003	$1,893,999	491	>100% Gain	$1,683,503
McGovern, James P (D-Mass)	$474,002	$2,673,503	$2,199,501	464	>100% Gain	$2,330,503
Cummings, Elijah E (D-Md)	$175,000	$887,506	$712,506	407	>100% Gain	$887,506
Harkin, Tom (D-Iowa)	$2,647,019	$13,373,057	$10,726,038	405	>100% Gain	$16,764,563
Conyers, John Jr (D-Mich)	$1,501	$7,500	$5,999	400	>100% Gain	$0
Faleomavaega, Eni F H (D-AS)	$77,007	$338,505	$261,498	340	>100% Gain	$48,004
Taylor, Gene (D-Miss)	-$32,500	$75,000	$107,500	331	>100% Gain	$32,500
Jackson Lee, Sheila (D-Texas)	$159,005	$615,506	$456,501	287	>100% Gain	$27,004
Costa, Jim (D-Calif)	$851,003	$3,073,002	$2,221,999	261	>100% Gain	$2,881,002

Name					>100% Gain	
Wyden, Ron (D-Ore)	$1,472,005	$4,817,513	$3,345,508	227	>100% Gain	$6,246,019
Christian-Christensen, Donna (D-VI)	$205,500	$625,501	$420,001	204	>100% Gain	$518,000
Bordallo, Madeleine Z (D-Guam)	$1,523,003	$4,565,002	$3,041,999	200	>100% Gain	$4,916,003
Kanjorski, Paul E (D-Pa)	$1,464,505	$4,356,505	$2,892,000	198	>100% Gain	$4,356,505
Spratt, John M Jr (D-SC)	$6,801,008	$19,543,006	$12,741,998	187	>100% Gain	$22,443,507
Watson, Diane E (D-Calif)	$48,501	$135,502	$87,001	179	>100% Gain	$111,002
Towns, Edolphus (D-NY)	-$269,497	$210,007	$479,504	178	>100% Gain	$214,506
Dodd, Chris (D-Conn)	$411,004	$1,139,508	$728,504	177	>100% Gain	$1,498,509
Dicks, Norm (D-Wash)	$261,504	$720,504	$459,000	176	>100% Gain	$698,003
Berman, Howard L (D-Calif)	$498,024	$1,367,020	$868,996	175	>100% Gain	$1,082,547

Name						
Visclosky, Pete (D-Ind)	$390,509	$1,064,511	$674,002	173	>100% Gain	$1,107,012
Higgins, Brian M (D-NY)	-$250,001	$170,505	$420,506	168	>100% Gain	$170,505
Brown, Corrine (D-Fla)	-$43,999	$28,001	$72,000	164	>100% Gain	$3,501
Schakowsky, Jan (D-Ill)	$71,008	$181,512	$110,504	156	>100% Gain	$188,511
Boren, Dan (D-Okla)	$591,502	$1,479,007	$887,505	150	>100% Gain	$1,002,507
Stark, Pete (D-Calif)	-$9,499,988	$4,295,508	$13,795,496	145	>100% Gain	-$11,542,496
Miller, Brad (D-NC)	-$462,997	$197,510	$660,507	143	>100% Gain	$210,015
Clyburn, James E (D-SC)	$165,504	$397,505	$232,001	140	>100% Gain	$397,005
Israel, Steve (D-NY)	-$104,000	$32,500	$136,500	131	>100% Gain	$0
Kennedy, Patrick J (D-RI)	$91,001	$207,501	$116,500	128	>100% Gain	$18,107,502

Dorgan, Byron L. (D-ND)	$289,011	$633,517	$344,506	119	>100% Gain	$765,019
Brady, Robert A (D-Pa)	$799,005	$1,641,004	$841,992	105	>100% Gain	$391,504
Ortiz, Solomon P (D-Texas)	$773,003	$1,563,006	$790,003	102	>100% Gain	$1,323,004
Kildee, Dale E (D-Mich)	$239,503	$481,004	$241,501	101	>100% Gain	$296,504
Totals for 41 Democrats	$10,019,43	$85,726,77	$75,707,34	756 %		$95,620,163

39 Republicans

Name						
LaTourette, Steven C (R-Ohio)	-$4,499	$590,502	$595,001	13,225	>100% Gain	$790,502
Chambliss, Saxby (R-Ga)	$16,001	$304,504	$288,503	1,803	>100% Gain	$297,003
Putnam, Adam H (R-Fla)	$724,510	$6,716,513	$5,992,003	1,754	>100% Gain	$6,453,513
McMorris Rodgers, Cathy (R-Wash)	$106,504	$1,423,013	$1,316,509	1,236	>100% Gain	$1,320,509
Pence, Mike (R-Ind)	$13,002	$158,007	$145,005	1,115	>100% Gain	$90,007
Rohrabacher, Dana (R-Calif)	$42,222	$463,504	$421,282	998	>100% Gain	$342,499
Culberson, John (R-Texas)	-$45,000	$337,501	$382,501	850	>100% Gain	$337,501
Inglis, Bob (R-SC)	$73,001	$571,513	$498,512	683	>100% Gain	$448,002

Name					
Mack, Connie (R-Fla)	-$242,000	$1,181,536	$1,423,536	588	>100% Gain	$1,287,536
Davis, Geoff (R-Ky)	-$19,995	$73,001	$92,996	465	>100% Gain	$73,001
McConnell, Mitch (R-Ky)	$3,072,514	$16,979,018	$13,906,504	453	>100% Gain	$19,929,018
Wicker, Roger (R-Miss)	$282,005	$1,526,508	$1,244,503	441	>100% Gain	$660,513
Thornberry, Mac (R-Texas)	$83,500	$391,001	$307,501	368	>100% Gain	$391,001
Shadegg, John (R-Ariz)	-$4,999	$12,501	$17,500	350	>100% Gain	$12,501
Ros-Lehtinen, Ileana (R-Fla)	$197,006	$874,005	$676,999	344	>100% Gain	$957,504
Ensign, John (R-Nev)	$1,041,795	$4,400,795	$3,359,000	322	>100% Gain	$4,054,202
Diaz-Balart, Lincoln (R-Fla)	$48,003	$172,005	$124,002	258	>100% Gain	$155,504
Poe, Ted (R-Texas)	$26,502	$88,504	$62,002	234	>100% Gain	$112,505

Name					>100% Gain	
Graham, Lindsey (R-SC)	$262,510	$801,009	$538,499	205	>100% Gain	$834,812
Myrick, Sue (R-NC)	$107,501	$306,003	$198,502	185	>100% Gain	$121,503
Sullivan, John (R-Okla)	$65,001	$183,001	$118,000	182	>100% Gain	$383,000
Blunt, Roy (R-Mo)	$223,003	$601,509	$378,506	170	>100% Gain	$765,009
Enzi, Mike (R-Wyo)	$518,011	$1,394,535	$876,524	169	>100% Gain	$1,692,536
Sessions, Pete (R-Texas)	$894,526	$2,407,019	$1,512,493	169	>100% Gain	$3,494,523
Barrett, Gresham (R-SC)	$1,004,004	$2,635,520	$1,631,516	163	>100% Gain	$2,536,518
Murkowski, Lisa (R-Alaska)	$516,515	$1,344,019	$827,504	160	>100% Gain	$1,366,020
Lucas, Frank D (R-Okla)	$403,004	$1,022,502	$619,498	154	>100% Gain	$1,010,502
Royce, Ed (R-Calif)	$121,004	$291,002	$169,998	141	>100% Gain	$315,004

Name				Rank		
Gohmert, Louis B Jr (R–Texas)	−$110,001	−$250,001	−$140,000	127	>100% Gain	$150,001
Forbes, J Randy (R–Va)	$441,901	$999,381	$557,480	126	>100% Gain	$805,480
Wilson, Joe (R-SC)	−$348,500	$78,515	$427,015	123	>100% Gain	$696,003
Bishop, Rob (R–Utah)	−$16,499	$3,501	$20,000	121	>100% Gain	$8,501
Burr, Richard (R–NC)	$506,011	$1,098,744	$592,733	117	>100% Gain	$1,375,888
Diaz-Balart, Mario (R–Fla)	−$65,001	$8,000	$73,001	112	>100% Gain	$32,500
Collins, Susan M (R–Maine)	$196,503	$410,005	$213,502	109	>100% Gain	$205,002
Garrett, Scott (R–NJ)	$97,501	$202,505	$105,004	108	>100% Gain	$338,005
Barton, Joe (R–Texas)	$39,502	$81,002	$41,500	105	>100% Gain	$81,002

⌐	McCaul, Michael (R–Texas)	$34,176,566	$69,619,248	$35,442,682	104	>100% Gain	$137,611,043
⌐	Aderholt, Robert B (R–Ala)	$780,510	$1,566,011	$785,501	101	>100% Gain	$3,927,511
⌐							
⌐	Totals for 39 Republicans	$45,223,644	$121,066,961	$75,843,317	168%		$195,473,184

And then you have to wonder why their staffers get such generous bonuses when they leave.
When a small business owner has to close down his business he doesn't even qualify for unemployment in a lot of states.

CHAPTER 4

EARLY VIRUSES THAT ENTERED GOVERNMENTS BLOODSTREAM

A HISTORICAL PERSPECTIVE TO LOBBYIST

No one seems to have the courage to appreciate and stand up for what was needed to keep the economy on track. Some of our presidents had the courage to stand up to monopolies and Lobbyist early in the formation of our country. They were willing to make great sacrifices to do what was right.

An example of lobbying or peddling influence was between President Andrew Jackson and Nicholas Biddle, a bank owner. Jackson viewed the bank as a hydra monster, buying editors and Congressman by the dozen for the purpose of corrupting the morals of the American people. Jackson felt the bank was using excessive powers over farmers, mechanics, and others not connected to the moneyed aristocracy.

He made a point to fight it, and even one who spoke eloquently to override a veto, Daniel Webster, had just asked Biddle for a twelve-thousand-dollar loan.

Even then, all you had to do was follow the money. In the end, Jackson was willing to take the chance of sacrificing his presidency to take on the lobbyist, and he won on both fronts.

During Teddy Roosevelt's terms, the lobbying became very serious. Mark Hanna wanted McKinley to win so much that he prodded big business to set aside a quarter percent of corporate assets for the McKinley campaign. He set a record of raising seven million dollars (equivalent to $143 million today). In 1901, Roosevelt wrote Congress that the Constitution framers had not seen the startling rise and grave evils of corporate monopolies. He ordered his Attorney General to sue the Northern Securities Company, the largest trust on earth. Roosevelt wanted to discipline these types of people to keep them from "buying" the unscrupulous politicians. *Presidential courage: brave leaders and how they changed America, 1789-1989* By Michael R. Beschloss

The incredible rapid growth of a virus(taxes) right under our noses.

"This gentleman puts things in a current perspective of how our current leadership is handling our government on our behalf and how they are paying for things."

-By Charlie Reese

Politicians are the only people in the world who create problems and then campaign against them.

Have you ever wondered, if both the Democrats and the Republicans are against deficits, WHY do we have deficits?

Have you ever wondered, if all the politicians are against inflation and high taxes, WHY do we have inflation and high taxes?

You and I don't propose a federal budget. The President does.

You and I don't have the Constitutional authority to vote on appropriations. The House of Representatives does.

You and I don't write the tax code, Congress does.

You and I don't set fiscal policy, Congress does.

You and I don't control monetary policy, the Federal Reserve Bank does.

One hundred senators, 435 congressmen, one President, and nine Supreme Court justices equates to 545 human beings out of the 300 million are directly, legally, morally, and individually responsible for the domestic problems that plague this country.

I excluded the members of the Federal Reserve Board because that problem was created by the Congress. In 1913, Congress delegated its Constitutional duty to provide a sound currency to a federally chartered, but private, central bank.

I excluded all the special interests and lobbyists for a sound reason. They have no legal authority. They have no ability to coerce a senator, a congressman, or a President to do one cotton-picking thing. I don't care if they offer a politician $1 million dollars in cash. The politician has the power to accept or reject it. No matter what the lobbyist promises, it is the legislator's responsibility to determine how he votes.

Those 545 human beings spend much of their energy convincing you that what they did is not their fault. They cooperate in this common con regardless of party.

What separates a politician from a normal human being is an excessive amount of gall. No normal human being would have the gall of a Speaker, who stood up and criticized the President for creating deficits. The President can only propose a budget. He cannot force the Congress to accept it.

The Constitution, which is the supreme law of the land, gives sole responsibility to the House of Representatives for originating and approving appropriations and taxes. Who is the speaker of the House? John Boehner. He is the leader of the majority party. He and fellow House members, not the President, can approve any budget they want. If the President vetoes it, they can pass it over his veto if they agree to.

It seems inconceivable to me that a nation of 300 million cannot replace 545 people who stand convicted -- by present facts -- of incompetence and irresponsibility. I can't think of a single domestic problem that is not traceable directly to those 545 people. When you fully grasp the plain truth that 545 people exercise the power of the federal government, then it must follow that what exists is what they want to exist.

If the tax code is unfair, it's because they want it unfair.

If the budget is in the red, it's because they want it in the red.

If the Army & Marines are in Iraq and Afghanistan it's because they want them in Iraq and Afghanistan.

If they do not receive social security but are on an elite retirement plan not available to the people, it's because they want it that way.

There are no insoluble government problems.

Do not let these 545 people shift the blame to bureaucrats, whom they hire and whose jobs they can abolish; to lobbyists, whose gifts and advice they can reject; to regulators, to whom they give the power to regulate and from whom they can take this power. Above all, do not let them con you into the belief that there exists disembodied mystical forces like "the economy", "inflation," or "politics" that prevent them from doing what they take an oath to do.

Those 545 people and they alone, are responsible.

They, and they alone, have the power.

They, and they alone, should be held accountable by the people who are their bosses.

Provided the voters have the gumption to manage their own employees.

We should vote all of them out of office and clean up their mess.

Charlie Reese is a former columnist of the Orlando Sentinel Newspaper.

What you do with this article now that you have read it is up to you. This might be funny if it weren't so true. Be sure to read all the way to the end:

Tax his land,
Tax his bed,
Tax the table,
At which he's fed.

Tax his tractor,
Tax his mule,
Teach him taxes
Are the rule.

Tax his work,
Tax his pay,
He works for
peanuts anyway!

Tax his cow,
Tax his goat,
Tax his pants,
Tax his coat.

Tax his ties,
Tax his shirt,
Tax his work,
Tax his dirt.

Tax his tobacco,
Tax his drink,
Tax him if he
Tries to think.

Tax his cigars,
Tax his beers,

If he cries
Tax his tears.

Tax his car,
Tax his gas,
Find other ways
Taxes to pass

Tax all he has
Then let him know
That you won't be done
Till he has no dough.

When he screams and hollers;
Then tax him some more,
Tax him till
He's good and sore.

Then tax his coffin,
Tax his grave,
Tax the sod in
Which he's laid...

Put these words
Upon his tomb,
'Taxes drove me
to my doom...'

When he's gone,
Do not relax,
Its time to apply
The inheritance tax.

Accounts Receivable Tax

Building Permit Tax

CDL license Tax

Cigarette Tax

Corporate Income Tax

Dog License Tax

Excise Taxes

Federal Income Tax

Federal Unemployment Tax (FUTA)

Fishing License Tax

Food License Tax

Fuel Permit Tax

Gasoline Tax (currently 44.75 cents per gallon) What? It was $3.59 at the BP in New Jersey this morning 8/2/2011

Gross Receipts Tax

Hunting License Tax

Inheritance Tax

Inventory Tax

IRS Interest Charges IRS Penalties (tax on top of tax)

Liquor Tax

Luxury Taxes

Marriage License Tax

Medicare Tax

Personal Property Tax

Property Tax

Real Estate Tax

Service Charge Tax

Social Security Tax

Road Usage Tax

Recreational Vehicle Tax

Sales Tax

School Tax

State Income Tax
State Unemployment Tax (SUTA)
Telephone Federal Excise Tax
Telephone Federal Universal Service Fee Tax
Telephone Federal, State and Local Surcharge Taxes
Telephone Minimum Usage Surcharge Tax
Telephone Recurring and Nonrecurring Charges Tax
Telephone State and Local Tax
Telephone Usage Charge Tax
Utility Taxes
Vehicle License Registration Tax
Vehicle Sales Tax
Watercraft Registration Tax
Well Permit Tax
Workers Compensation Tax
Exit Tax (when you move out of New Jersey, LOL!!!)

And since he wrote this we will bet there have been no less than 10-20 more new taxes.

And after all of these taxes here is how they are influenced and where they are spending it and putting our futures in jeopardy.

In 1992, the ten largest political action committees (PACs), ranked by total dollars given to candidates for the House, were realtors, at $2.95 million; American Medical Association, $2.94 million; Teamsters, $2.44 million; trial lawyers, $2.37 million; National Education Association (teachers union), $2.32 million; United Auto Workers, $2.23 million; AFSCME (public employee union), $1.95 million; National Automobile Dealers, $1.78 million; National Rifle Association, $1.74 million; and letter carriers, $1.71 million.

Using a chart of House committees, one easily sees the committees these PACs look to for legislation in their favor or for blocking legislation that might harm them. The realtors look to banking and commerce, the doctors to all committees dealing with health care, the teamsters to labor and commerce. The teamsters win the "Mom, Flag, and Apple Pie" award for their PAC name. It doesn't mention teamsters; it's the "Democratic, Republican, Independent Voter Education Committee."

Here is a quick analysis of what it is being spent by the government. As always, Government is not being held accountable.

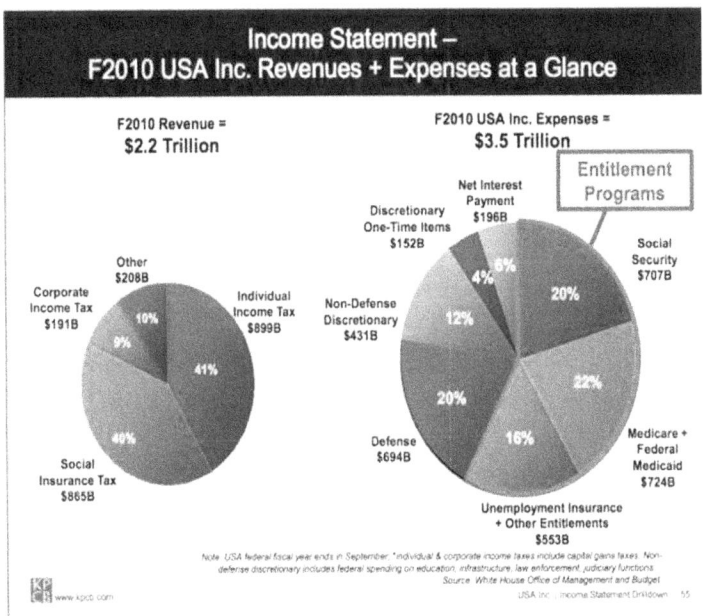

Income Statement –
F2010 USA Inc. Revenues + Expenses at a Glance

F2010 Revenue =
$2.2 Trillion

F2010 USA Inc. Expenses =
$3.5 Trillion

Entitlement Programs

Other $208B
Corporate Income Tax $191B
Individual Income Tax $899B
Social Insurance Tax $865B

Net Interest Payment $196B
Discretionary One-Time Items $152B
Non-Defense Discretionary $431B
Defense $694B
Social Security $707B
Medicare + Federal Medicaid $724B
Unemployment Insurance + Other Entitlements $553B

Note: USA federal fiscal year ends in September. "Individual & corporate income taxes include capital gains taxes. Non-defense discretionary includes federal spending on education, infrastructure, law enforcement, judiciary functions
Source: White House Office of Management and Budget

USA Inc. Income Statement Drilldown   55

"I wish it were possible to obtain a single amendment to our constitution - taking from the federal government their power of borrowing." Thomas Jefferson, 1798

It's not very pretty and getting worse by the minute. This was in March 2011. The debt is growing at $58,000.00 per second. That is $3.5 million each minute.

"U.S. Debt Tops $14.3 Trillion for First Time"

Monday, April 18, 2011
By Terence P. Jeffrey

(CNSNews.com) - The national debt has passed another historical milestone, topping $14.3 trillion for the first time ever, according to data released by the U.S. Treasury late Monday afternoon.

When the Treasury opened for business on Friday, April 15, according to the Treasury's **Bureau of the Public Debt**, the national debt stood at $14.27 trillion ($14,270,792,119,184.89). By the close of business Friday, the debt had climbed to $14.31 trillion ($14,305,336,580,992.11), an increase of $34.54 billion ($34,544,461,807.22).

Friday's $34.54-billion jump in the national debt almost equaled the $38.5 billion the Republican House leadership said would be cut from spending for the remainder of this fiscal year by the continuing resolution that the Congress passed on Thursday and President Obama signed Friday.

The federal government is now perilously close to hitting its legal limit on debt.*1

Congress is now asking to raise the debt ceiling again.

Which party has had control of Congress the longest since 1945 and holds the responsibility for our debt?

Early Viruses That Entered Governments Bloodstream

U.S. PRESIDENT	PARTY	TERM YEARS	START DEBT/GDP	END DEBT/GDP	INCREASE DEBT ($T)	INCREASE DEBT/GDP (IN PERCENTAGE POINTS)	HOUSE CONTROL (WITH # IF SPLIT DURING TERM)	SENATE CONTROL (WITH # IF SPLIT DURING TERM)
Roosevelt/ Truman	D	1945–1949	117.5%	93.1%	0.05	-24.4%	79th D, 80th R	79th D, 80th R
Harry Truman	D	1949–1953	93.1%	71.4%	0.01	-21.7%	D	D
Dwight Eisenhower	R	1953–1957	71.4%	60.4%	0.01	-11.0%	83rd R, 84th D	83rd R, 84th D
Dwight Eisenhower	R	1957–1961	60.4%	55.2%	0.02	-5.2%	D	D
Kennedy/ Johnson	D	1961–1965	55.2%	46.9%	0.03	-8.3%	D	D

President	Party	Years							
Lyndon Johnson	D	1965–1969	46.9%	38.6%	0.05	-8.3%	D		D
Richard Nixon	R	1969–1973	38.6%	35.6%	0.07	-3.0%	D		D
Nixon/ Ford	R	1973–1977	35.6%	35.8%	0.19	+0.2%	D		D
Jimmy Carter	D	1977–1981	35.8%	32.5%	0.28	-3.3%	D		D
Ronald Reagan	R	1981–1985	32.5%	43.8%	0.66	+11.3%	D		R
Ronald Reagan	R	1985–1989	43.8%	53.1%	1.04	+9.3%	D		99th R, 100th D
George H. W. Bush	R	1989–1993	53.1%	66.1%	1.40	+15.0%	D		D
Bill Clinton	D	1993–1997	66.1%	65.4%	1.18	-0.7%	103rd D, 104th R		103rd D, 104th R

Bill Clinton	D	1997–2001	65.4%	56.4%	0.45	-9.0%	R	R
George W. Bush	R	2001–2005	56.4%	63.5%	1.73	+7.1%	R	107th Split, 108 R
George W. Bush	R	2005–2009	63.4%	83.4%	2.63	+20.0%	109th R, 110th D	109th R, 110th D
Barack Obama	D	2009–	83.4%				111th D, 112th R	D

Source: CBO Historical Budget Page and Whitehouse FY 2011 Budget, Table 7.1, Federal Debt at the End of Year PDF, http://www.senate.gov.

It looks like the Democrats win that contest hands down. They held the majority and set the agenda, therefore they are responsible for the results.

Facts don't lie.

A lot of people would like to blame the President or his Administration. We have to be real here. The one person at the top can be involved in arm twisting, but at the end of the day, 545 other votes make the difference.

As the American public, we all need to hear some common sense and realism. We may not like it, and when you see all of these polls the media and government would have us believe, we are evenly divided.

We do not believe that.

There is a vast majority that can deal with common sense. We are fearful, because we have been lied to for so long.

'A country in which 42% of the population is totally mis-informed is not a country where democracy is safe."

-- Paul Craig Roberts

WE THOUGHT RIGHT HERE WE SHOULD GIVE THE SMALL BUSINESS CHOICE FOR PRESIDENT A CHANCE TO MAKE HIS CASE FOR HIS BID FOR THE JOB.

There are four boxes to be used in defense of liberty: Soap, Ballot, Jury, and Ammo.

Please use in that order.

AMERICA NEEDS A CANDIDATE WITH THIS PLATFORM!!

I HAVE DECIDED TO BECOME A WRITE-IN CANDIDATE FOR PRESIDENT IN THE YEAR 2012. HERE IS MY PLATFORM:

(1) Any use of the phrase: "Press 1 for English" is immediately banned! English is the official language; speak it or wait outside of our borders until you can.

(2) We will immediately go into a two year isolationist attitude in order to straighten out the greedy big business posture in this country. America will allow no imports, and we'll do no exports. We will use Wal-Mart's policy (You know small business disagrees with this(: "If we ain't got it, you don't need it." We'll make it here and sell it here!

(3) When imports are allowed, there will be a 100 percent import tax on it coming in here.

(4) All retired military personnel will be required to man one of the many observation towers located on the southern border of the United States (six-month tour). They will be under strict orders not to fire on south-bound aliens.

(5) Social Security will immediately return to its original state. If you didn't put nuttin' in, you ain't getting nuttin' out. Neither the president nor any other politician will be able to touch it.

(6) Welfare. Checks will be handed out on Fridays, at the end of the forty-hour school week, the successful completion of a urinalysis test for drugs, and passing grades.

(7) Professional Athletes. Steroids? The first time you check positive you're banned from sports for life.

(8) Crime. We will adopt the Turkish method, i.e., the first time you steal; you lose your right hand. There are no more life sentences. If convicted of murder, you will be put

to death by the same method you chose for the victim you killed: gun, knife, strangulation, etc.

(9) One export of ours will be allowed, wheat, because the world needs to eat. However, a bushel of wheat will be the exact price of a barrel of oil.

(10) All foreign aid, using American taxpayer money, will immediately cease and the saved money will help to pay off the national debt and, ultimately, lower taxes. When disasters occur around the world, we'll ask the American people if they want to donate to a disaster fund and each citizen can make the decision as to whether, or not, it's a worthy cause.

(11) The Pledge of Allegiance will be said every day at school and every day in Congress.

(12) The National anthem will be played at all appropriate ceremonies, sporting events, outings, etc.

My apology is offered if I've stepped on anyone's toes.... nevertheless.....

GOD BLESS AMERICA!

Sincerely, Bill Cosby

CHAPTER 5

FIRST DIAGNOSES OF ILLNESS AND WHY THE SBA WAS FORMED

Not since the interstate road system has there been the kind of devastation to the small businesses health. All the small businesses built up in and around the small towns and on the rural roads before the interstates were built as bypasses around them. Of course everyone then recognizes that the traffic that was once passing by these businesses was now going around.

This was about the time the same time the Government created the Small Business Administration.

Is important to know how one government agency got started: Small Business Administration.

As banks grew, their interest in loaning to small business did not. The risk versus the return was not worth it for them. The time it took to make and service the loan was not enough return for them. *Currently only around 10% of the 3000 banks even will loan SBA money.*

The U.S. Small Business Administration (SBA) was established on July 30, 1953, by the United States Congress with the passage of the Small Business Act. Its function was to "aid, counsel, assist and protect, insofar as is possible, the interests of small business concerns."

What is a small business?

The Office of Advocacy defines a small business as an independent business having fewer than 500 employees. The definition of "small business" used in government programs and contracting varies by industry.

2. How important are small businesses to the U.S. economy?

Small firms:

- Represent **99.7 percent of all employer firms**.
- Employ half of all private sector employees.
- Pay 44 percent of total U.S. private payroll.
- Generated **65 percent of net new jobs** over the past 17 years.
- Create more than half of the nonfarm private GDP.
- Hire 43 percent of high tech workers (scientists, engineers, computer programmers, and others).
- Are 52 percent home-based and 2 percent franchises.
- Made up 97.5 percent of all identified exporters and produced 31 percent of export value in FY 2008.

- Produce 13 times more patents per employee than large patenting firms.

Source: U.S. Dept. of Commerce, Census Bureau and Intl. Trade Admin.; Advocacy-funded research by Kathryn Kobe, 2007.

3. How many small businesses are there?

In 2009, there were 27.5 million businesses in the United States, according to Office of Advocacy estimates. The latest available Census data show that there were 6.0 million firms with employees in 2007 and 21.4 million without employees in 2008. Small firms with fewer than 500 employees represent 99.9 percent of the total (employers and nonemployers), as the most recent data show there were about 18,311 large businesses in 2007.

Source: Office of Advocacy estimates based on data from the U.S. Dept. of Commerce, Census Bureau, and trends from the U.S. Dept. of Labor, Bureau of Labor Statistics, Business Employment Dynamics.

4. What is small firms' share of employment?

Small businesses employ about half of U.S. workers. Of 120.6 million nonfarm private sector workers in 2007, small firms employed 59.9 million and large firms employed 60.7 million. About half of small firm employment is in second-stage companies (10-99 employees), and half is in firms that are 15 years or older. Small firms' share of employment in rural areas is slightly higher than in urban areas; their share of part-time workers (22 percent) is similar to large firms' share (19 percent). Small firms' employment share remains steady since some small firms grow into large firms over time.

Source: U.S. Dept. of Commerce, Census Bureau: Statistics of U.S. Businesses, Current Population Survey and Business Dynamics Statistics; and the Edward Lowe Foundation

5. What share of net new jobs do small businesses create?

Small firms accounted for 65 percent (or 9.8 million) of the 15 million net new jobs created between 1993 and 2009.

Much of the job growth is from fast-growing high-impact firms, which represents about 5-6 percent of all firms and are on average 25 years old.

Source: U.S. Dept. of Labor, Bureau of Labor Statistics, Business Employment Dynamics; Advocacy-funded research by Zoltan Acs, William Parsons and Spencer Tracy, 2008

Employment size of enterprise	Firms
Firms with no employees (as of March 12)	*802,034*
Firms with 1 to 4 employees	*2,777,680*
Firms with 5 to 9 employees	*1,043,448*
Firms with 10 to 19 employees	*632,682*

Firms with 20 to 99 employees

526,355

Firms with 100 to 499 employees

86,538

Firms with 500 employees or more

17,047

Firms with 500 to 749 employees

5,695

Firms with 750 to 999 employees

2,709

Firms with 1,000 to 1,499 employees

2,828

Firms with 1,500 to 2,499 employees

2,281

Firms with 2,500 employees or more

3,534

Firms with 2,500 to 4,999 employees

1,739

Firms with 5,000 to 9,999 employees

905

Firms with 10,000 employees or more

890

Source: U.S.Dept. Of Commerce, Census Bureau: Statistics of U.S. Businesses, Current Population Survey and Business Dynamics Statistics; and the Edward Lowe Foundation

Even by the government numbers, *5.8 million (5, 8000, 000) firms have 499* or fewer employees. This versus *37,000 thousand over 500* puts things in perspective when it comes to hiring opportunities. The larger companies (more than five hundred employees) have taken over the higher percentage of hiring.

What this shows and proves is that the larger companies are putting the smaller companies out of business and making it harder and harder for them to find niches. All the while they are sending the work overseas and they are removing more niches and hiring opportunities as well.

5,800,000.00 firms (up to 499 employees) X 3 employees= 17,400,000.00 new hires

25451.00 firms (up to 1,000 employees) X 50 employees= 1,272,550.00 new hires

5109.00 firms (up to 2500 employees) X 150 employees=510,900 new hires

2644 firms (up to 10,000 employees) X 1500 employees=3,966,000.00 new hires

890 firms (over 10,000 employees) X 3500 employees=3,115,000.00 new hires

If you study the numbers it is quick to see what is the most realistic and you have to know that we never want to rely on the large companies and the government to do the hiring.

Always remember the "Devil is in The Details."

For a small business the amount of new customers and new business that it takes to hire a new employee is quite a bit. While the large companies are doing business with other large companies it makes it even harder for small business especially since the niches are getting harder to find. The disturbing trend shown by the Governments numbers is that Small business hiring has been in a decline for a while.

The bottom line is that small business are getting sicker and we felt the need to write this will and get it distributed to as many people as possible.

Below are the facts of what impact the small businesses have on the economy.

Small Business Impact on the Economy

The estimated 29.6 million small businesses in the United States:

- Employ just over half of the country's private sector workforce
- Hire 40 percent of high tech workers, such as scientists, engineers and computer workers
- Include 52 percent home-based businesses and two percent franchises
- Represent 97.3 percent of all the exporters of goods
- Represent 99.7 percent of all employer firms
- Generate a majority of the innovations that come from United States companies

Source: U.S. Small Business Administration Office of Advocacy, September 2009

The Governments idea of starting up new small business is throwing $30 billion at the SBA. When budget cuts are discussed (when was the last time any were really cut) they discuss cutting the staff of the SBA.

It's not realistic to even believe that trimming the SBA staff by half is going to be able distribute the money to the banks to distribute to small businesses. Below is copied right from the SBA website. This is just (1) list of the forms that could be filled out.

We are sure you would have no problem wading through it to get a loan or why there are only a very few banks that want to swim in these waters.

The SBA is taking some pretty impressive new initiatives to help small businesses; the problem as always is that for whatever the reason they are avoiding the real problem.

The Big Businesses and their major contributions to all political parties and politicians is netting the same results. NO NEW JOBS. When you admit that the creator of jobs is starting up to 70% of all new jobs. Right after that you give full reign to the exact parties that kill the opportunities and the momentum; you are either stupid or have a different plan in mind.

Try to stay focused now and drink a lot of coffee or one of those 5 hour drinks that are supposed to give you energy.

Here is what small business has to go through to borrow money from the government through a bank that will do it.

They say they have reduced the SBA paperwork to what the Banks use as paperwork. We would suggest you start calling and see how many banks would even talk to you.

U.S. Small Business Administration

First Diagnoses of Illness and Why the SBA was Formed

SBA FORM #	FORM NAME	VERSION #	FILE SIZE	UPDATED DATE
--	CDC Quarterly Delinquency Report	2-9-2009	1.54 MB	02/27/2011 - 19:09
--	Offer In Compromise (OIC) Tabs	10/2011	--	10/11/2011 - 13:59
--	Servicing and Liquidation Actions 7(a) Lender Matrix	8	103.99 KB	09/15/2011 - 17:00
--	7(a) Risk Based Lender Review	--	34.06 KB	02/27/2011 - 19:09
--	504 Risk Based Lender Review	10.01.09	33.39 KB	02/27/2011 - 19:09
--	Lender Checklist for Submitting PLP Loan Requests	4/11	327.91 KB	03/30/2011 - 15:46
--	Authorization (Community Express Loan)	10/19/04	27 KB	02/27/2011 - 19:09
--	Authorization (SBA Express/Patriot Express Loan)	--	32 KB	03/08/2011 - 14:48

	Document	Date	Size	Timestamp
--	7(a) Submission Instructions and Checklist	November, 2011	--	11/08/2011 - 16:24
--	Request for Loan Reinstatement	--	83.5 KB	02/27/2011 - 19:09
--	Transfer of Participation Agreement	--	41.5 KB	02/27/2011 - 19:09
--	Power of Attorney Agreement	--	27.91 KB	02/27/2011 - 19:09
--	General Liquidation Instructions	1/29/2008(b)	391.5 KB	02/27/2011 - 19:09
--	Care and Preservation of Collateral (CPC) Tabs	--	231.25 KB	05/26/2011 - 13:24
--	NGPC CPC Status and Payment Statement	--	35 KB	05/26/2011 - 13:04
--	SBA Charge Off Procedures Summary & Suggested Wrap-Up Report	6/16/2010	209.58 KB	05/26/2011 - 13:00
--	Litigation Plan	--	51 KB	05/26/2011 - 13:14

--	Regular 7(a) Guaranty Purchase Package Tabs	10/2011	352.77 KB	10/06/2011 - 13:21
--	10 Tab Express Purchase Demand Kit	--	788.08 KB	05/26/2011 - 13:27
--	10 Tab Express Purchase Demand Kit with ARC Loan provisions	--	1.49 MB	05/26/2011 - 13:36
--	Pre-Application Review Request	08/2008	30 KB	02/27/2011 - 19:09
--	Eligibility Information Required for 504 Submission	09/30/11	794.34 KB	10/04/2011 - 17:25
--	CDC Checklist for Submitting a 504 Loan Application	10/2010	26 KB	02/27/2011 - 19:09
--	CDC Checklist for Submitting Real Estate Appraisal	08/2008	31.5 KB	02/27/2011 - 19:09
--	CDC Checklist for Submitting Environmental Investigation	02/2011	19.85 KB	10/24/2011 - 20:13

CDC Checklist for Submitting Equipment Appraisal	08/2008	30.5 KB	02/27/2011 - 19:09	--
Reinstatement of SBA Guaranty	--	42.5 KB	02/27/2011 - 19:09	--
CDC 503/504 Liquidation Plan	--	170 KB	02/27/2011 - 19:09	--
Protective Bid Analysis Exhibit A	--	36 KB	02/27/2011 - 19:09	--
CDC 504/503 Litigation Plan	--	48 KB	02/27/2011 - 19:09	--
Forms A-9 through A-12: Budget Detail Worksheet	--	52.76 KB	05/26/2011 - 13:20	--
Template for TA Narrative Report	--	35.85 KB	05/26/2011 - 12:27	--
Model Debenture SBIC, L.P. (Model Partnership Agreement)	2.0	118.78 KB	05/26/2011 - 13:06	--
Fresno CLC Letter	--	519.6 KB	02/27/2011 - 19:09	--

First Diagnoses of Illness and Why the SBA was Formed

:|	Little Rock CLC Letter	:|	520.64 KB	02/27/2011 - 19:09
:|	Request to Honor SBA 7(a) Loan Guaranty	:|	98.16 KB	05/26/2011 - 13:39
:|	7(a) Eligibility Questionnaire	November, 2011	:|	11/22/2011 - 17:21
:|	503/504 Liquidation Wrap Up Report	:|	37.5 KB	03/10/2011 - 16:33
:|	Debit Authorization (SBICs)	:|	23 KB	04/07/2011 - 09:58
:|	CDC/504 Supplemental Information for Processing	02/2011	133.57 KB	10/26/2011 - 22:11
:|	CDC/504 Supplemental Information for Processing	02/2011	133.57 KB	10/26/2011 - 12:16
1050	Settlement Sheet (Use of Proceeds Certification)	10-08	760.91 KB	05/11/2011 - 10:52
1059	SBA Form 1059: Security Agreement	2-04	104.2 KB	03/08/2011 - 14:11

1059	SBA Form 1059: Security Agreement	2-04	17.58 KB	03/08/2011 - 14:11
1062	Small Business Development Center Counseling Record	11-00	52.35 KB	03/21/2011 - 12:08
1065	Applicant Licensee's Assurance of Compliance (Public Interest)	12-08	20.01 KB	04/07/2011 - 09:32
1081	SBA Form 1081: Statement of Personal History for Non-bank Lenders, CDCs and Micro-Lenders	4-10	1.05 MB	03/08/2011 - 17:55
1086	Secondary Participation Guaranty Agreement	2-11	796.2 KB	03/31/2011 - 09:05
1128	Guaranty Loan Purchased	5-86	51.64 KB	03/07/2011 - 06:17
1149	Lender's Transcript of Account	6-08	588.81 KB	03/07/2011 - 06:23

We thought looking at this one (1) form to be filled out might give you an indication of why both Banks and small businesses go to the SBA as a last resort. This is 1 of about 20-30 forms necessary depending on the type of business.

Go ahead get more coffee it will be over soon.

==
=

SBA ELIGIBILITY QUESTIONNAIRE FOR STANDARD 7(a) GUARANTY

This questionnaire is a tool to assist lenders in making basic eligibility determinations. For more information on loan

Eligibility, please refer to SOP 50 10 5(D).

If eligibility is questionable, please contact the Standard 7(a) Loan

Guaranty Processing Center (LGPC) at (877) 475-2435 or 7aquestions@sba.gov.

Please note: All final eligibility determinations are made by SBA, not the lender.

If any statement below is checked "False", the loan is ineligible or requires additional information and clarification.

I. General Information -- Complete the following:

Applicant Name

Lender Name

Describe Type of Business

Purpose of Loan

TRUE FALSE

The products and/or services of the applicant business are available to the general public.

This loan will benefit the small business.

The applicant does not discriminate with respect to goods, services, or accommodations

offered based on race, color, religion, sex, marital status, handicap or national origin of a

person or fail or refuse to accept a person on a non-segregated basis as a customer.

II. Ineligible Businesses -- Certain business types are ineligible for SBA assistance.

A non-profit business.

Primarily engaged in lending.

A passive business owned by developers or landlords that do not actively use or occupy the assets acquired or improved with the loan proceeds that is not an Eligible Passive Company discussed below (e.g. shopping center) .

A life insurance company (life insurance agents, however, may be eligible).

Located in a foreign country or owned by undocumented aliens.

Selling through a pyramid or multi-level sales distribution plan.

Deriving more than one-third of gross annual revenue from legal gambling activities . Engaged in any illegal activity.

Restrict patronage for reason other than capacity.

A government-owned entity (a small business owned or controlled by a Native American tribe may be eligible if the business is a legal entity separate from the tribe).

Principally engaged in teaching, instructing, counseling, or indoctrinating religion or religious beliefs .

A consumer or marketing cooperative (producer cooperatives may be eligible).

Earning more than 1/3 of its gross annual revenue from packaging SBA loans.

Business with an associate who is incarcerated, on probation, on parole, or has been indicted for a felony or a crime of moral turpitude.

Business in which the Lender or any of its associates owns an equity interest.

Business which presents live performances of a prurient sexual nature or derives more than 5 percent of its gross revenue from the sale of products or services, or the presentation of any depictions or displays of a prurient sexual nature.

Business that has defaulted, or has a principal who has defaulted, on a Federal loan or Federally-assisted financing resulting in the Federal government sustaining a loss, (unless waived by SBA for good cause) . Primarily engaged in political or lobbying activities. Speculative in nature (such as a shopping center developer, oil wildcatting, or primarily engaged in R&D)

The Small Business Applicant is not one of the above ineligible business types. TRUE FALSE

If "False", the loan is ineligible.

==

__This was only a few pages into at least a 40-50 page application. We were sure you would get the point in a hurry and would not want to see the rest of the 1 form.__

This article came out early in the current administration. Continue to remember this not based on any partisan blame.

"New program aims to help lend money"

Now don't take it that nothing is getting done at all. Here is a program being instituted by the federal government.

"I'm thrilled to be here on what is an exciting day," said the President as he prepared to sign the Small Business Jobs Act this afternoon. With small business owners who will receive tax breaks and better access to credit in the audience, the President explained to everybody why he has fought so long for it:

This is important, because small businesses produce most of the new jobs in this country. They are the anchors of Main Street. They are part of the promise of America—the idea that if you've got a dream and are willing to work hard, you can succeed. That's what leads a worker to leave a job to become her own boss. That's what propels a basement inventor to sell a new product or an amateur chef to open a restaurant. It's this promise that has drawn millions to our shores and made our economy the envy of the world.

These words are true, but will the government actually show the effort to see the initiatives succeed? Where are the results?

This next article shows how important all the earlier effort for small business was to them.

Uncle Sam's Great Recession stimulus for small businesses may soon be over. The SBA faces a 45 percent decrease in funding, as part of President Obama's 2012 proposed budget.

The proposed SBA budget stands at $985 million for 2012, down from the $1.8 billion the SBA received in 2010 and fueled in large part by $962 million in supplemental stimulus appropriations that were designed to boost small-business loans. Those appropriations are no longer available for 2012.

Other areas slated for budget cuts include **Small Business Development Centers**, which provide support and mentoring to entrepreneurs, and administrative costs, including a $7 million drop in salaries and expenses.

We find it interesting that the Government announce these new initiatives and then in no time propose to cut the budget to admin-istrate the SBA in half.

It is like saying we have the surgeon to operate on you but because of budget cuts he has to do in the dark so we can save on power.
All of this is based on appropriating less than 1 percent of the budget to the very group that does most of the hiring.
The article that follows does a good job of summing up what the government proposal through the SBA would do for small business.

CHAPTER 6

No One Is
Spending Money

- "Small Business to Obama: Tax Cuts Won't Work"
  By Deborah Solomon
- This is another well intentioned initiative by
  the government that has not been thought out
  and will not help small business and then in
  turn not help the economy.
- The Obama administration has targeted small
  business with laser-like focus, pushing a $30
  billion small-business lending fund in Congress
  and, later this week, rolling out a tax break
  allowing businesses to deduct 100% of qualified capital investments.

But the chief economist at the National Federation of
Independent Businesses said today that small business
doesn't need more tax relief. Instead, he said, Washington

should aim its firepower at consumers so they begin spending money and creating demand for the products and services small companies provide.

"If you give a small business guy $20,000 he'll say, 'I could buy a new delivery truck but I have nobody to deliver to,'" said William Dunkelberg, chief economist for NFIB.

Rather than aim more tax relief at business, Dunkelberg said Washington should extend the Bush-era tax cuts for everyone – including those making above $250,000.

"History shows that letting Washington have the money and spend it is very ineffective," he said.

The administration's latest idea, which would allow businesses to temporarily deduct 100% of "qualified" capital investments, can help "on the margin," Dunkelberg said. With capital-spending by small business at a 35-year low, some firms will naturally take advantage of a temporary tax incentive to replace products. But Dunkelberg said he thinks most small businesses will hold on to their cash until more certain economic times.

We differ in opinion slightly with author of the above article in that the consumer cannot be addressed if they don't have a job. You cannot use the services of a small business if you have no money to spend if you have no job.

The best way to help, he said, is to "finally address the most important person in the economy – the consumer."

We think this blog recently really summed things up well. As a matter of fact they nailed it and this book is proving it.

As a seasoned small business attorney, I cannot agree more with this commentary on the US government's treatment of one of the essential pillars of the US economy. I can attest to the fact that small business owners are credit starved and deprived. I have watch bankers (both the big ones and the community ones) restrict, shut down and cut off small business lines of credit, even in cases when the business was not in default of the loan terms. The bankers claim it is because the collateral (which generally includes all the business' assets, the owners' personal guarantees, and any other unencumbered assets the bankers can get their hands on). No SBA program works because the SBA only guarantees their loans; it does not make loans in the form businesses need. Only about 10% of the 3,000 or so US banks participate in the SBA programs, the SBA loan paperwork is often more demanding that the commercial banks' forms, the process of applying, complying, and generally trying to speak to anyone at the SBA with even a modicum of knowledge is a half-day marathon of patience. If this administration doesn't stop passing worthless legislation and start focusing on small business' real issues (i.e., access to reasonable capital, reducing regulatory compliance, and lessening the tax burden), the economy may soon consist of only a dozen or so giant corporations.

There is another place to look to discover how the small businesses are doing and how it looks for the future. Visit the markets that they go to buy for their stores. Ask the suppliers how their seasons have been. If they are honest they will share that they have gotten no better at all.

If small businesses are not spurring new start-ups, unemployment stays high. People cannot purchase much with food stamps and unemployment checks.

Federal grant would encourage small businesses to borrow from banks.

By Kirsten Valle Pittman

kpittman@charlotteobserver.com

Posted: Saturday, Feb. 19, 2011

Small-business owners interested in the N.C. Capital Access Program can learn more and apply for loans through their lenders. Participating lenders are responsible for approving loans, setting terms and deciding reserve fees.

Although NC-CAP is meant to attract borrowers who might not qualify under conventional standards, they must meet lenders' borrowing requirements. Among the qualities lenders will look for: good credit, a solid business plan, sufficient investment in the business, collateral and the ability to repay.

A new effort to ease lending for small businesses could help create hundreds of thousands of jobs, state officials said Friday.

Banks, credit unions and other lenders, which participate voluntarily, determine which borrowers fit the program and set the loan terms. The lenders will provide loans of up to $5 million that come with a 2 percent to 7 percent fee, depending on the risk, to be paid by the borrower and lender.

During the two years the government money is available, he expects NC-CAP to spur $800 million in loans and 200,000 jobs, he said.

Where are the results?

This is a good article with good intentions, but the flaws are as follows:

- *The bank officers making the decisions to make the loan have no experience in what it takes to start a business.*
- *The amount of money being lent to each small business is typically not enough to help the entrepreneur have the time to see an idea or product come to market.*
- *They want more collateral than any small business would have at the start or at the time of expansion.*
- *The most needed element that is not present is the type of expertise that counsels and works with the small business owners to help them succeed after the money is loaned.*

To summarize, few institutions are seeing the value in small business, but even those don't know how to follow up and help nurture the small business to succeed.

The following articles show how employment in the United States is leaning toward government.

If you want to understand better why so many states—from New York to Wisconsin to California—are teetering on the brink of bankruptcy, consider this depressing statistic: Today in America there are nearly twice as many people working for the government (22.5 million) than in all of manufacturing (11.5 million). This is an almost exact reversal of the situation in 1960, when there were 15 million workers in manufacturing and 8.7 million collecting a paycheck from the government.

It gets worse. More Americans work for the government than work in construction, farming, fishing, forestry, manufacturing, mining and utilities combined. We have moved decisively from a nation of makers to a nation of takers. Nearly half of the $2.2 trillion cost of state and local governments are the $1 trillion-a-year tab for pay and benefits of state and local employees. Is it any wonder that so many states and cities cannot pay their bills?*Mr. Moore is senior economics writer for The Wall Street Journal editorial page*.

The reason for this is very simple. Small Business is being exterminated and nothing is being done to stop it so the Government is having to hire to hide this information.

A CURRENT BUSINESS VIRUS THAT IS CAUSING STAGE 1 TO SPREAD QUICKER AND COULD SHORTEN THE LIFE OF SMALL BUSINESS

If these conditions continue they could be deadly to the economy.

Statistics show that over the last few decades, the new jobs created by small business and new small business has fallen from 85 percent of all new hires to well below that.

- If the trend continues, we will be left with larger companies, and the government to do all the hiring. The net effects will be less and less new small business startups.
- If you stifle over 85 percent of new hiring by small business, you are choking the economy. Unemployment will continue to rise and will last longer.
- You will then have a large unemployed who cannot find a job and who deserve the opportunity to who

are tired of pulling money out of their retirement accounts.

- These unemployed workers cannot spend on consumer goods in general, and all businesses in order to survive will have to lower prices to try and survive.
- The businesses will not show profits and begin to feed off each other. This forces them to copy other company's product lines and begin price wars.
- In turn, the businesses will have to lay off more workers and cannot pay back bank loans. This is happening now.
- The banks will not show a profit and continue the making layoff and not making loans.
- Foreclosed homes and office space will not sell or rent. This will create a back log of even more unsold homes. You then have affected the Real Estate industry even worse.
- People will not be able to afford insurance of any kind. This affects the medical industry. People without money and jobs cannot pay medical bills.
- The government will have no tax revenue. It will then have to convince us that they have the money to bail out more industries, and extend unemployment benefits even longer.

During this last meltdown, we not only loaned to our banks and bailed out large companies here, we loaned a lot of money overseas, which our government hid from us.

God forbid that these circumstances come together, but if you paid attention to over the past two to three years, you saw a number of these events happening.

The way out is *not* for large companies or government to get larger. We cannot afford to be putting all our eggs in one basket with larger companies, or a larger government, as an employer.

Creation of new small businesses and new jobs is the answer.

STAGE TWO(2) OF SMALL BUSINESS ILLNESS

Once Companies of all types reached a certain size they quit doing buisness almost entirely with small buisness.

They have been consumed by getting bigger and bigger and then they chose to do buisness with companies who supply to them that are large as well.

Why has it become so difficult for small businesses to work with mega-companies?

A historical perspective always seem to help.

In the 1920s and 1930s, large chain store operations extended their reach throughout the United States. Competing with smaller "mom-and-pop" grocery and drug stores, the chains frequently benefited from economies of scale and was able to sell at prices lower than those of their smaller rivals. Responding to this threat to small businesses, a number of states passed legislation heavily taxing chain stores, and Congress enacted the Robinson-Patman Act of 1936 and the Miller-Tydings Act of 1937 to shield small retailers from the competition of larger firms.

Mansel Blackford explains pretty clearly how our government allowed the larger companies to encroach on small companies.

The importance of small business to the development of America's business system and cultural values carried over into the political realm as well. Small businesses have often received special treatment in state and national legislation.

A major reason for the enactment of America's first antitrust laws, the Sherman Act in 1890 and the Clayton Act in 1914 was a generalized desire to protect small firms from the perceived "unfair" encroachments of larger companies, even though the larger businesses were usually more efficient in their production and distribution of goods to consumers.

Most recently, Congress created the SBA in 1953 as a federal government agency charged with the goal of encouraging small business development in the United States and, through the Regulatory Flexibility Act of 1980 and other measures, exempted small firms from many aspects of federal government regulation of business.

However, the expressed desires of Congress and the state legislatures usually have not succeeded. In fact, some of the legislation—the Sherman Act and, perhaps, the Robinson-Patman Act—*has aided larger concerns at the expense of smaller ones, and other pieces of legislation designed to help small firms have been largely ineffective.* Moreover, actions of the federal government, such as its defense procurement policies, have often favored large businesses over small ones.

Thus, a paradox has existed.

Americans have generally admired the owners of small businesses and have desired the preservation of small enterprises, even at the expense of economic efficiency.

Nonetheless, governmental policies have often directly or indirectly furthered the development of big businesses in the United States. There has been a discrepancy between political rhetoric and reality, one that continues to the present day. *** *Mansel G. Blackford History of Small Business in America*

OK so let's see if we can get this right the first time. You admire us, we have done more for the economy and hiring than all the large companies put together but you just stood by and let the large companies get larger. I'm sure our readers know by now that you are pandering to the lobbyist and special interest groups and are personally responsible for driving the economy in the ditch.

So to explain in common sense terms what happened from our vantage point here is what happened.

1. The small companies did not work in larger demographic areas.
2. The larger consolidated company could leverage the larger portfolio of business for less cost.
3. The large companies did not want to be staffed to work with the small businesses in multiple areas (They consolidated their purchasing departmen- They have looked to outsource jobs to other countries for services that would have created more jobs in the United States. Every one of these jobs could have been filled by a local worker, but not at the low wages paid overseas.
4. The Tarp money being spent by the Government is by in large going to large companies who use large vendors and unions.

If the small business could not grow into a large regional or national company they were ignored.

Out of fairness some companies had to grow larger or go out of business.

Also some chains stores and restaurants are not all company owned, they allow some local ownership.

This lack of control through Stage 2 is what led to the explosion in Stage 3.

CHAPTER 7

THE INVASION OF THE BIG BOX AND CHAIN STORES

THE METASTASIZING OF THE DISEASE TO STAGE THREE (3)

THE BIG BOX CHAIN STORES AND MONOPOLIES GROWTH.

When the first Big Box Chain Store arrives it clears all vegetation and wildlife, reroutes any water on the property, and leaves a beautiful visual of concrete, asphalt parking lots and a clear view for a short time of nothing but dirt, before other chain stores of all sizes join them.

These illustrations show the impact that the big-box chain stores are having on small business. The devastation is like a nuclear bomb (some would like to say that this is too graphic, whatever it takes to wake people up), and as others hit, they each have their own blast wave or small business "kill zone." In this picture, the first big-box store is there, the land has been cleared for the others to follow. That land is not cleared for growing corn and other vegetables. Each big-box store and chain stores have a devastating effect on small business in the surrounding area.

We are speaking of the current environment. It does not have to continue nor is it irreversible. Given the current economy, it is not going to continue at the recent pace of growth in America.

Recently the press for the Corporate Mega boxes has been that there profits are down. It seems that they are looking overseas for their new growth and profits. ***So much for the global economy and their bragging about creating local jobs.***

The net effects of these large box stores expansion is that they push small businesses out completely or they have to move which puts more pressure on survival because of cost to relocate and maintain a client base. When the first one hits, it has a blast zone that differs in each town and county but it can range from 2 miles to 25 miles, and all small business that have any overlapping products with the chain stores feel the impact. After that, the small business in that area will either have to find a complete new niche or close down.

After they hit, medium-box and chain stores of all kinds and sizes follow as well, and then all types of other chain stores.

When you get outside of these blast zones, you find family-owned small businesses in almost every category. The service and the prices are great.

In a lot of these chain stores the personal service is a thing of the past. They can't because they are under staffed. They know that customers are too lazy to drive around to other stores to shop around. They don't have to worry about customer service as much until their business is off and then you will see for a short period people trying to be more helpful. Buyers have been indoctrinated into believing that because the items are all under one roof, we must be saving money. Here is the inevitable result!

The majority of the for lease signs that you see around are from small businesses that have either gone out of business or had to move because of the cost of space. If you look in those same areas you still see the big box and other chains. They have the funds to weather the economic storms.

The small business company usually pays higher wages and is better for their communities. They are in most cases have been permanent fixtures in the community and have a vested interest in the community's success.

The big box stores try to say that they provide jobs, but the number they have put out of work is far greater than the number that they hire. They also hire part-time, pay few benefits, and manage and control the hours they work. (If you don't think they control hours, just ask some of the employees or watch a shift change or try to find someone to help you) These major companies have the money to develop automation and systems that reduce jobs from the corporate office to the field.

These automated systems are putting more people out of work and on unemployment more than anyone realizes or wants to admit. The problem affects almost every type of consumer product: clothing, office supplies, furniture, accessories, restaurants, appliances, auto parts, gas stations, hardware, and many more.

Is there real competition here? There might be between other big-box stores of the same type.

Watch the reactions when the largest of these big-box stores continue to diversify and start to have a negative impact on the other larger chain stores.

What will happen when big box stores go into banking and expand their automotive departments, or diversify into other chains' business lines and compete against the mid-size box stores with their purchasing power?

They already cross more lines than many people would imagine.

All you have to do is walk through a big-box store and look for the items that were once in small businesses and specialty stores. The suppliers are now selling their products to anyone who will order them. All you have to do is look around and you see all of these big box stores continuing to carry more and more product that in a lot of cases has nothing to do with their core business.

It really becomes more apparent when these new smart phones have an application that read bar codes and the pricing and tells you where you can buy it cheaper.

Small business cannot compete in this environment.

Take a look in some of the Home Improvement stores and try and explain why some of the items they are selling have anything to do with Home Improvement.

It has to be obvious that selling dog collars and dog food as well as coffee has nothing to do with fixing up your home.

Competition has made its way down to small businesses with small suppliers. Suppliers used to protect their customers in certain ZIP codes; now they will sell to the store across the street. This creates price wars, which causes more small businesses to die, and guess what's left?

In the long haul, these super big box stores as well chains stores are going to be feeding on themselves.

When you kill small business you are taking away both the entity that hires and produces the workers with the income who would possibly shop in their stores as well. If you keep killing your only source of food, when you get hungry you will do dumb things.

You can see by this image how all of the other chain stores develop around them (the "blast zone"). This is what we call the secondary destruction area of the first blast zone. Some would call it growth.

When you inspect this blast zone, you notice a lot of the same chain store names but also, neighborhoods, apartment housing, and schools being built around these malls.

You see the same chain names over and over. What happens is the developers are building the customer base for these chains right next to them. If you also notice the areas that have not been cleared you can bet that it is either been zoned or will be zoned for these stores.

The older neighborhoods are one of the places that small businesses continue to have a chance to have a place to fill niche. Even there, the big stores look for a way to creep in.

One of the final blast zones in the image below shows the expansion after the second wave. As you can see, the area is much larger and includes a lot more chains of all types. The housing developments gets larger, and the area attracts more chain buisnesses, which pushes the opportunities and cost to do business for the small start-up company further out.The sprawl itself, with the zoning, chains,and housing, limits small business even more.

When you see the massive growth of these corporations you have to see the difficullty for the small business to compete. We have all heard that in real estate it is about location,location,location. These groups can afford that and small buisness cannot.

The numbers speak for themselves. Wal- Mart was by no means the first big-box chain, but its size and impact blows everyone before, and the current competition, out of the water. Pictures are worth a thousand words. 3176 stores and counting.

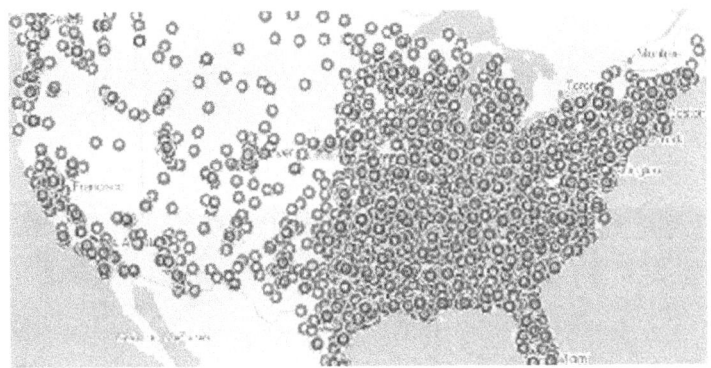

Wal Marts

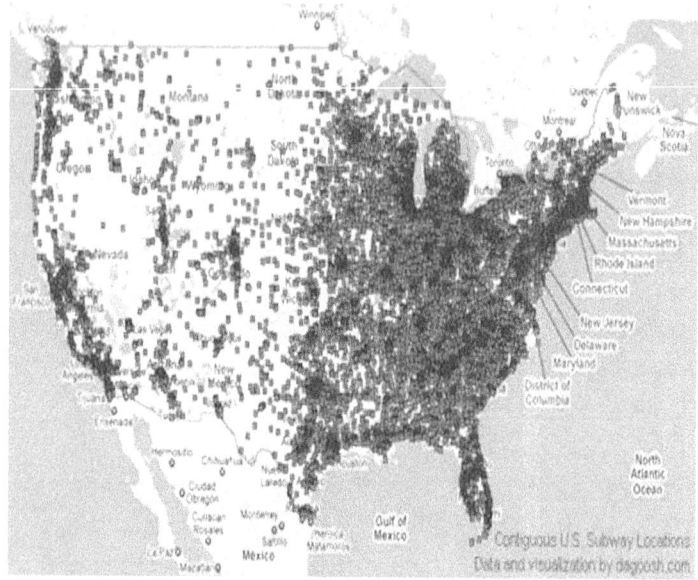

Subway 30,000+

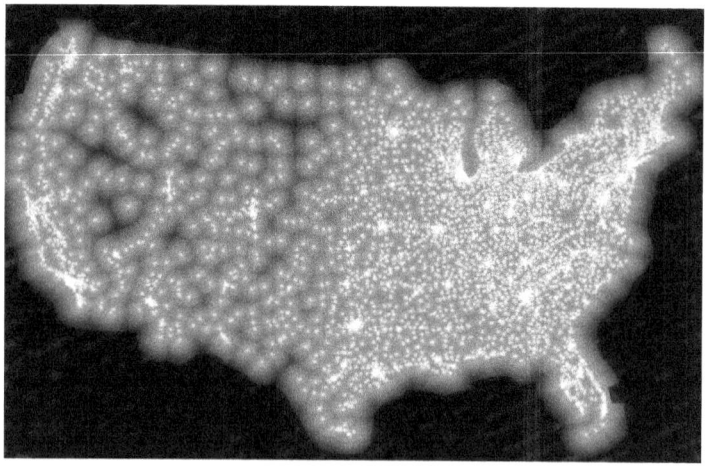

McDonalds over 14,000

Burger King 7398

Pizza Hut 6171

In the US today there are as you can see more than 70,000 chain restaurants.

Numbers don't lie and neither do pictures and facts.

Drive to any strip mall and look at the names of the store and restaurants and see if they aren't the same ones you see everywhere else.

Besides the incredible amount of For Lease signs that used to be small businesses we thought it might be interesting to list some of the names that we are sure you will recognize.

Wal-Mart
Home Depot
Lowes
Sears
Kmart
Taco Bell
Hardees
Starbucks
Kentucky Fried Chicken
Wendy's
Bo jangles
Advance Auto
Arbys
Circuit City
Staples
Fridays
Ruby Tuesdays
Dollar General
Family Dollar
Target
Walgreen
Rite Aid
Harris Teeter

Food Lion
IGA
Borders
7-11
BP
Woolworths
Sam's Club
Costco
Dollar Tree
Kohl's
Belk
Dillard's
Macys
Nordstrom's
Federated
Hecht's
Marshall Fields
Nieman Marcus
Saks
TJ Max
Burger King
Blimpies
Fuddruckers
Denny's
Dominoes
McDonalds

This is just a short list but you can get the idea of what we mean when one of the big box store lands that in all cases all or most of the chains mentioned above will be right behind. What we want everyone to wake up to the fact that this is choking off and destroying the hiring engine (Small Business) of our economy.

There is no doubt they hire but the numbers are showing that they are putting more out of work than they are hiring.

If we could do an overlay map you would be able to see what our earlier pictures show in the way of eliminating the opportunities for the small business entrepreneur. This includes almost every type of business there is.

While you're at it, drive around the surrounding community, and see how many local restaurants and local stores there are, along with going-out-of-business signs and rental signs.

Entrepreneurs are fighters and will fight on until their last breath, but even they need help in their corner once in a while. Small business niches are getting harder and harder to find.

Some people would like to call this whining or sour grapes. Not one of you has ever had to sacrifice to make a payroll so you really have no basis to make the comment. The key point is we shop in their stores as well. All small business is looking for is a level playing field and when these big boxes see that a product is selling well in a small business they do not need to offer in their stores as well.

You have to see the pattern of these stores and their development. You also can't believe that any small business can compete or stand in their way.

While they are running over small buisness the unemployed are left on the sideline.

Over time, the blast zones almost eliminate most of the opportunites for small businesses.Small business can still find niches from time to time but they are few and far between.

The article below describes what the big-box stores, chain stores, or malls have done to small businesses. The basic premise supports what we have said: the authors are trying to make the case that a Wal-Mart brings a lot of other retailers and therefore adds to the expansion and employment base.

Think about our blast zone analogy. They are basically admitting they are killing small business and their opportunities.

IS WAL-MART SMOTHERING SMALL TOWN AMERICA?

Entrepreneurial Executive, Annual, 2005 by Rachel R. Entenza, Balasundram Maniam, Hadley Leavell

ABSTRACT

Everywhere there is evidence of new establishments being built. It seems that cities are now reaching out further and small towns growing up overnight. Some call it progress; others call it sprawl. One of the most recognizable faces popping up in the new development is the brainchild of Sam Walton, the founder of Wal-Mart. New Wal-Marts *are being constructed as currently estimated at the rate of one a day.* These superstores invite strong feelings pro and con and the effect of their presence is much debated. The purpose of this paper is to examine the effects of the discount superstore entering into a community.

INTRODUCTION

Is Wal-Mart an example of the great American dream or a small town nightmare? It is difficult to travel far without finding a Wal-Mart looming on the horizon bustling with shoppers scrounging to save money. Founded in 1962 in Bentonville, Arkansas by entrepreneur Sam Walton, Wal-Mart has grown into a commercial superpower offering products and services in a one-stop shopping format that may include: automotive service, banking, fast food, optometry, photography, and hair and nail salons. Wal-Mart provides low-cost shopping for the cash- strapped consumer. However, the question continues as to whether the end result is positive or negative when Wal-Mart locates a store, which can sometimes be over 200,000 square feet, on the edge of town.

Proponents of the mega-superstore cite the creation of new jobs, lower-priced goods and increased city revenue as benefits. However, many people in the communities are convinced its presence will have negative effects on the smaller, existing community "mom and pop" stores, and lead to the dissolution of a unique small-town atmosphere. Studies as to the effects of introduction of big-box retailers, those with merchandising establishments over 100,000 square feet, have been conducted in various regions with conflicting results. This study will analyze those previous studies and also the various viewpoints for and against the introduction of large discount superpowers into a community. Emphasis will be placed on the introduction of Wal-Mart as it is currently the United States' largest retail establishment. There will also be some discussion as to how currently operating small businesses can perhaps adapt to doing business in the shadow of the giant.

LITERATURE REVIEW

The debate about large retail establishments entering communities is not a new one. Authors have been discussing this issue for almost forty years. "Reactions of a Small Town to a Rumored Discount House," was written in 1965 with many of the same arguments regarding Sears and A&P that are now being voiced about Wal-Mart.

Kenneth Stone researched the introduction of Wal-Marts into Iowa, with data collected on the resulting impact on the host town, non-Wal-Mart towns, cities and small towns. The most comprehensive study done regarding the effect of a discount superstore is "Impact of Wal-Mart Stores on Iowa Communities: 1983-1993."

"The premise of the study is that in areas of somewhat static population (such as in states like Iowa) the size of the retail 'pie' is relatively fixed in size for a geographical area. Consequently, when a well-known national chain like Wal-Mart opens a large store in a comparatively small town, it invariably will capture a substantial slice of the retail pie. The end result is that other merchants in the area will have to make do with smaller slices of the retail pie, or get out of business. In areas of the country where the population is growing rapidly, there is room for more retail establishments and the effect will be diluted considerably" (Stone, 1995).

Unsurprisingly, Stone's findings support the argument that the introduction of a Wal-Mart into a town has a negative impact on already existing businesses resulting in the demise of the pre-existing businesses. ***

We see their points, but in general, feel that this article is old and soft-peddles the devastating effects that the big-box stores are having on small businesses.

It looks like some things are coming full circle.

Look at the date of this article. If this should not be a wakeup call that the stuff that they are doing is causing this problem then what is.

WAL-MART: OUR SHOPPERS ARE 'RUNNING OUT OF MONEY'

Wal-Mart CEO Mike Duke (left) speaking to a gathering of industry watchers in New York on Wednesday. By Parija Kavilanz, senior writer April 28, 2011: 10:43 AM ET

NEW YORK (CNNMoney) -- Wal-Mart's core shoppers are running out of money much faster than a year ago due to rising gasoline prices, and the retail giant is worried, CEO Mike Duke said Wednesday.

"We're seeing core consumers under a lot of pressure," Duke said at an event in New York. "There's no doubt that rising fuel prices are having an impact."

Wal-Mart shoppers, many of whom live paycheck to paycheck, typically shop in bulk at the beginning of the month when their paychecks come in.

Lately, they're "running out of money" at a faster clip, he said.

- Americans have generally admired the owners of small businesses and have desired the preservation of small enterprises, even at the expense of economic efficiency.

- Nonetheless, governmental policies have often directly or indirectly furthered the development of big businesses in the United States. There has been a discrepancy between political rhetoric and reality, one that continues to the present day. ***Mansel G. Blackford History of Small Business in America.

- We all saw how the "too big to fail" idea fell on its butt. If Big Box and Chain stores continue in the direction you are going, they may just find out how that feels.

Here is what big-box stores, chain restaurants with their healthy food and buying in bulk have done for us. Remember Laughter is still the best medicine!!

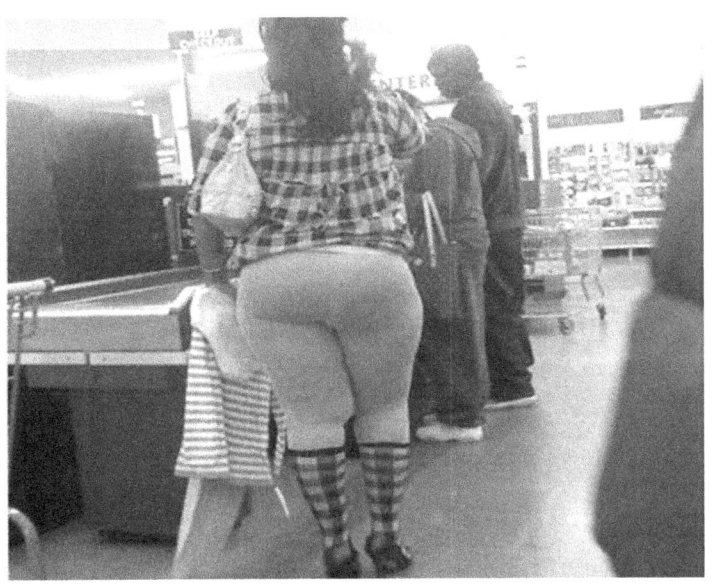

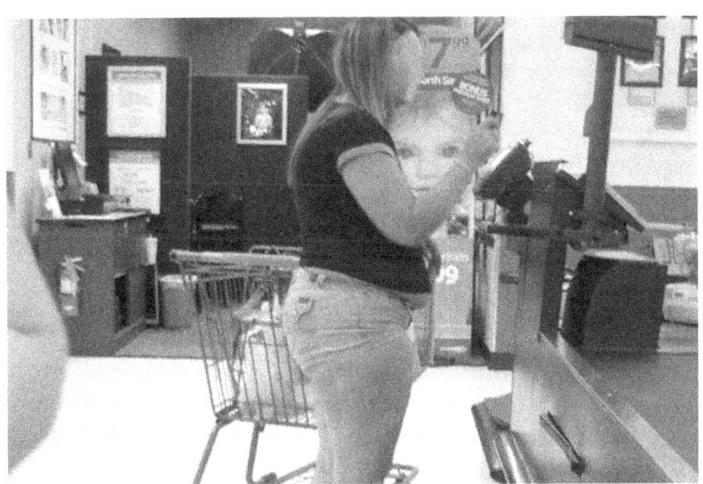

We are made to believe that these stores make our life simpler, but because we are buying in bulk, **the price we are paying is killing our economy**.

We better open our eyes quick, or maybe we should close them.

BIG-BOX STORES

Big-box stores have been stomping on small business, and the tougher times get the more they will destroy as many businesses as it takes for them to survive.

The following article proves our point. If Big Box business falls off, they increase the diversity of their product line and lower their prices. This hurts small business even more and puts pressure on the other big-box stores.

WAL-MART'S READY TO DO BATTLE ON PRICES

"What has made Wal-Mart great over the decades are 'every- day low prices' and our {product} assortment," he said. "We got away from it."

Now, with its strategy of low prices all the time back in place, Duke said making Wal-Mart a "one-stop shopping stop" is a critical response to dealing with the rising price of fuel.

Addressing that challenge, Duke said the company made mistakes by shrinking product variety and not being more aggressive on prices compared to its competitors. ** (see our point?)

Wal-Mart CEO. By Parija Kavilanz, senior writer April 28, 2011: 10:43 AM ET

This will create an environment that will cause a higher unemployment. Companies with over 5000 employees seem to be currently handling close to half of the economy's employment, and the government is handling a large portion as well. This is a dangerous scenario.

Look in the tags or on the labels of chain stores items and see where the products are made. Almost every one of the big box stores is buying their goods from overseas. They are sending jobs overseas and then they wonder why their customers do not have the money to shop with them.

We need find it interesting that they are killing small business and sending the very jobs overseas of the people who might shop with them. This is what is referred to as cutting your nose off to spite your face.

It has been said that buying American would create close to 200,000 jobs immediately.

The destruction of your shopping customer base on purpose can't seem to be smart even to the Wall Street wizards.

There is always a plan underway for the Big Box Stores to get bigger and diversify. Grow or die.

THE CRASH OF
THE HOUSING INDUSTRY

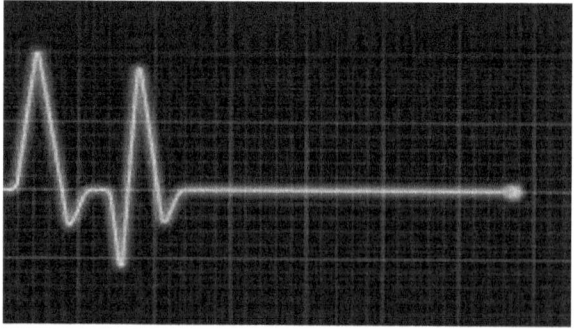

Was it Fatal?

When the housing industry went into its boom it created probably more small businesses than any other industry in the last 50 years. When the housing bubble burst, this had a devastating effect on small businesses as well as employment.

Congress was responsible.

The Community Reinvestment Act also created a lot of the illegal immigration problem, and once again, we got to see government at its worst. When the economy crashed, one party of congress wanted illegal immigrants to stay around for the unemployment and welfare benefits so that they would vote for their party. The other party wanted them to go home or go through the process of becoming legal citizens. When the work dried up, the majority of illegal immigrants went home anyway.

If you had a chance to go into some of these new homes on the market during the peak of home values, you would have seen in a $350,000 home, some plastic furniture, a mattress on the floor, a 50-inch flat-screen TV on the wall, and a brand-new SUV in the driveway. That was not someone planning to live there for long and just someone spending the fake equity.

A good example follows:

FBI agents broke up a $4 million house-flipping ring in Queens made up of Bangladeshi immigrants. Conspirators recruited straw buyers (**Straw buyers** are people who consent that their names and personal details are used by certain people with the purpose of obtaining mortgage loans with no purpose of ever inhabiting these homes.) to buy properties in Jamaica and Richmond Hill using false identities. The buyers applied for credit cards to improve their

credit ratings, and then filled out loan applications with fraudulent employment and income data. The ring bought and sold homes to pump up appraised values. One two-family residence in Jamaica changed hands four times in two years, rising from $395,000 to $745,000 before ending up in foreclosure. BY ROBERT GEARTY
DAILY NEWS STAFF WRITER

The voters need to make all the Congresspersons that pushed the Community Reinvestment Act (CRA) and their staffs move into these abandoned and foreclosed homes and use them for offices.

Was the CRA good intentioned or was there another purpose? The banks did not have the guts to tell the government to stick it. The people running Freddie Mac and Fannie Mae should be roommates with Bernie Madoff.

Thomas Jefferson said in 1802:
"I believe that banking institutions are more dangerous to our liberties than standing armies. If the American people ever allow private banks to control the issue of their currency, first by inflation, then by deflation, the banks and corporations that will grow up around the banks will deprive the people of all property - until their children wake-up homeless on the continent their fathers conquered".
Thomas Jefferson was brilliant!
Small businesses were affected in that small custom builders were either bought out or run off, for the most part, by large track home builders during the ramp up and rapid growth of the housing boom.

The same consolidation that went on happened with the builders happened with the vendors that supported them, like roofers, hvac companies, sheetrock companies etc. The vendors that supported the builders had to get larger or go out of business as well.

This resulted in a lot of small businesses leaving and eliminating the opportunity for new ones to start up.

A by-product of this disaster has been the number of very qualified people who were laid off after this who are still looking for work or had small businesses during the consolidation phase and are very qualified to start another one but cannot do so.

An additional problem that hit small business was the consolidation or roll up of the residential and commercial real estate businesses. You saw the same roll up with the large track home builders.

Now realtors have had to follow the foreclosure notices caused by the groups mentioned. One of the unfortunate consequences of all of this is that the same realtors who were selling a lot of nice homes to some very qualified people are now having to chase foreclosed properties and doing short sales while seeing people who are qualified being turned down by the same banks that were throwing money at everyone a few years ago.

Here is the description for a real estate short sale.

A **short sale** is a sale of real estate in which the proceeds from selling the property will fall short of the balance of debts secured by liens against the property and the property owner cannot afford to repay the liens' full amounts, whereby the lien holders agree to release their lien on the real estate and accept less than the amount owed on the debt. Any unpaid balance owed to the creditors is known as a *deficiency*. Short sale agreements do not necessarily release borrowers from their obligations to repay any deficiencies of the loans, unless specifically agreed to between the parties.

A short sale is often used as an alternative to foreclosure because it mitigates additional fees and costs to both the creditor and borrower; however both will often result in a negative credit report against the property owner.

They are now giving awards to a person who handles the greatest number of short sales.

When it comes to foreclosures, what the government, banks, and lawyers are doing to people is criminal and should be stopped. They set up this environment, and the blood is on their hands. They allowed it and are profiting from it. No matter how you look at it, it's wrong.

If you go to the websites of some of the large mortgage companies, you will see a feature to click on if you want help in redoing your loan (for a substantial fee and interest rate). Below it, you will likely see a link to review foreclosed properties for sale. Surely even they have to see how this looks to the public.

The government and financial institution are watching people being thrown out of their homes. With no conscious they are making a profit off of it. This is a crime beyond description.

Freddie Mac, the taxpayer-owned mortgage giant, has placed multibillion-dollar bets that pay off if homeowners stay trapped in expensive mortgages with interest rates well above current rates.

Freddie began increasing these bets dramatically in late 2010, the same time that the company was making it harder for homeowners to get out of such high-interest mortgages.

No evidence has emerged that these decisions were coordinated. The company is a key gatekeeper for home loans but says its traders are "walled off" from the officials who have restricted homeowners from taking advantage of historically low interest rates by imposing higher fees and new rules.

Freddie's charter calls for the company to make home loans more accessible. Its chief executive, Charles Haldeman Jr., recently told Congress that his company is "helping financially strapped families reduce their mortgage costs through refinancing their mortgages."

But the trades, uncovered for the first time in an investigation by ProPublica and NPR, give Freddie a powerful incentive to do the opposite, highlighting a conflict of interest at the heart of the company. In addition to being an instrument of government policy dedicated to making home loans more accessible, Freddie also has giant investment portfolios and could lose substantial amounts of money if too many borrowers refinance.

"We were actually shocked they did this," says Scott Simon, who as the head of the giant bond fund PIMCO's mortgage-backed securities team is one of the world's biggest mortgage bond traders. "It seemed so out of line with their mission."

The trades "put them squarely against the homeowner," he says.

It would be interesting to see some of the bankers, lawyers, and Congressmen experience losing a house, especially when they are responsible for causing the loss. Reading articles about this, and seeing the maps of where people profit from it, is just sick. They will not experience it because they are being paid so much. Or their net worth is growing so rapidly (remember earlier chart of growing net worth?) while everyone else has to take money out of their 401-k. and have the job security that the rest of us don't have.

The hard-working person who loses a home and credit is devastated.

It has gotten to the point that some cities are tearing down recently built abandoned houses that were foreclosed on because of what they are doing to the other housing values in the same neighbor hoods. The banks have quit paying property taxes on them and will not maintain them and then will not even pay to have them torn down.

Once again, looking out for everyone but the homeowner.

A man is not an orange. You can't eat the fruit and throw the peel away.

ARTHUR MILLER, *Death of a Salesman*

RESORT TOWNS.

CURRENT TEMPORARY BIG BOX AND CHAIN STORE IMMUNITY ZONES.

Some resort towns have the vision and courage to protect their small business. They are few and far between

Some of the most charming coastal and historic towns are now letting cruise ships into their cities. The chains are following them, and you guessed it, say goodbye to small businesses.

This article below shows how big these boats (or should we say floating cities) are.

This cruise ship weighs 160,000 tons, it is 1,112 feet long (almost ¼ miles long), 184 feet wide and it has 15 passenger decks holding 3,634 guests double-occupancy. Freedom of the Seas towers 208 feet tall, approximately the same height as two of the Statue of Liberty, placed head to toe.

A brand new feature's the H2O Zone, or the "spray ground" which has colorful fiberglass sculptures shooting jets of water, geysers shooting from the ground and water cannons. There's even a lazy river and waterfall inside! At night, this area, with the integration of an incredible lighting system, will be transformed into a sculpture garden. Royal Caribbean says, "There's nothing like the H2O Zone on any other cruise ship today."

Another first-ever feature is a dedicated sports pool located in the main pool area. One of the two pools of the Freedom of the Seas is used almost exclusively for athletic pool games, ranging from basketball and volleyball to synchronized swimming.

Located at the heart of this largest cruise ship, the Royal Promenade is a 445-foot-long *shopping, dining* and entertainment boulevard that spans the length of an entire football field. At night, the Promenade hosts street parades, put on by select staff, commencing from a revolutionary new descending bridge amidst a fanfare of music, lasers and lights. Guests can also enjoy relaxed reading at the 3,600-volume Book Nook.

With all those amenities, why would they need to dock at a town? Do they need to dump their waste? (We know they do that out at sea, oh goodie anyone for some seafood?)

We would bet that all contractors servicing the boats except for the tugboats are national contractors.

Why bring a city (the Cruise Ship) to a city with all of these amenities? It already has a shopping mall on it. We get it; they bring all these people to shop at the chain stores. People in wind suits and fanny packs don't buy from the family businesses because the products might cost ten cents more. This is typically true for tour buses as well to the other resort towns with the same results. The shopping customers are looking for the chain discount stores.

The cruise ship companies have tried to bring the cruise ships into some of the greatest little islands, and thank God the reefs and channels are too shallow, or they would spoil them as well. They have tried to dredge the channels, but nature filled them back in faster than they could dredge them. It was cost prohibitive—they would have had to raise the all-you-can-eat buffet price by $5.

We also see that they may be having trouble finding qualified help to drive these boats.

If boats can't get to the islands, the developers swoop in on Caribbean islands that have been unspoiled. You get to see how far the governments there will let the developers go in taking away their charm.

Now here is a quick quiz for you. Why do the governments allow the developers and the large retail companies to come to their towns and islands?

Time's up.

They want the tax revenue because they have built the bureaucracy around themselves to protect their job. In most cases, there are small businesses there, and when the developers get there, these disappear. You have to see the trend of small businesses progressing illness continuing.

Think of the words to the song "Big Yellow Taxi," sung by Joni Mitchell: "They paved paradise to put up a parking lot." Maybe that should be parking deck, because they make more money off a deck.

OTHER RESORTS TOWNS

The other Small Resort Towns have to fight daily to prevent the developers from destroying the charm and character of their towns.

All it takes is a few chains such as hotels, restaurants and retail stores and there goes small business. It does not have to always be the big box stores.

But even the small local governments are building their employee base to protect their jobs and really don't care about the small business. They only care where the next tax dollar comes from.

Constantly you will see these specialty strip centers and you will find some really unique small businesses but they typically anchored with chains stores and inevitably the boutiques go under. Some people would like to say that customer traffic is drawn by the chains, we beg to differ, and they can find those anywhere.

THE LOOMING DEADLY VIRUS

Do these towns exist? Absolutely! Would a big-box store plant itself dead in the middle of it? You can bet your

on it.

Big Box Stores and Chain Stores would have us believe that when they bring their new development into a region, it is creating new jobs, a new tax base, and new wealth for the employees. This is not true. The unemployment goes up in that community. All they have done is kill small business, take away motivation, and destroy niches for the future.

SMALL BUSINESSES OVERSEAS

If we want to see protection of entrepreneurs, you are going to have to look at other countries. If you have ever been to Europe, you will see business after business owned by the entrepreneur. You can find things there that you can't find anywhere else, and the suppliers typically do not sell to Big Boxes.

This will be our next book - *"The looming takeover of Europe's Small Business by the Mega Stores."* Once we have killed the Small business in America we will conquer the rest of the world.

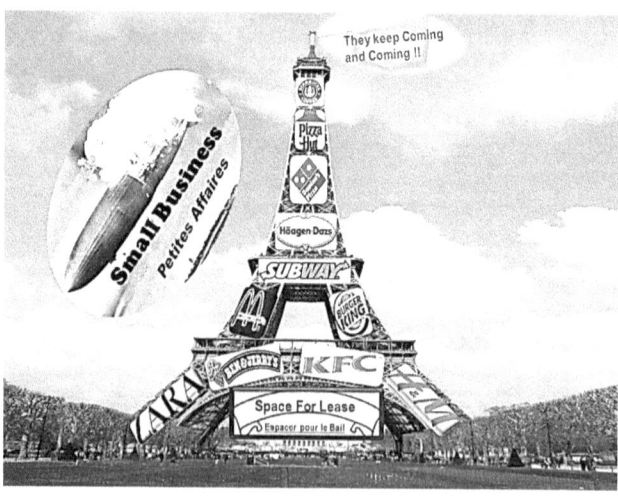

Europeans have some chains, but for now the small businesses are more prevalent. Will they be protected or will they lose their charm as well? The chains are creeping in and are pushing more and more of the family businesses out.

It seems like some Countries like South Korea and Germany are saying no to some of the Big Boxes. Maybe they are smart enough to recognize what these companies do to their economies. Some more will find out the hard way.

ONE OF THE RAPID CARRIERS
OF THE DISEASE

BANKING DEREGULATION AND
INTERSTATE BANKING

The information below discusses banks and their ability to operate across state lines, as well as work investment houses, in the 1930s. When that was altered, we saw a "too big to fail" attitude. What did that cost us in the recent bailout of a trillion dollars? It was the taxpayer's money, and the government will have us believe that it has been paid back. Show us the money.

Businesses had no choice but to be small in America's early days. Transportation was slow and inefficient, keeping markets too fragmented to support large-scale enterprise. Financial institutions also were too small to support big business. And productive capacity was limited because wind, water, and animal power were the only sources of energy. Whatever the reason businesses were small, Americans liked it that way.

Small business, they believed, cultivates character and strengthens democracy.

As Thomas Jefferson, the third president of the United States, put it, a nation of farmers and small businesspeople would avoid dependence, which "begets subservience and venality, suffocates the germ of virtue, and prepares fit tools for the designs of ambition. "Christopher Conte Small Business in U.S. History

These true and powerful words have obviously been forgotten. The fallout from this will be debated by the so-called experts for years. The banks wanted to loan more money to only the larger companies and make bigger deals, and investment houses became only interested in creating mergers and acquisitions. Companies saw the consolidation of departments and productivity, equipment and computers, and then would lay off employees. All along the way, the financing of small businesses was almost completely overlooked, because it would not make enough profit. The hiring engine was once again being exterminated.

This next article describes the wisdom in our business early leaders when they saw the need to keep banks from consolidating across state lines. Think about the competition between community banks for small businesses accounts if the banking rules had been left in place this is when the mega banks started.

Banking, indeed the whole financial services industry, is in a state of transition. The distinctions among the various financial entities--banks, savings and loan associations, insurance companies, real estate brokers, securities broker-dealers, finance companies, and investment brokers--are blurring. The reasons for this are manifold. Technology, such as automated teller machines and other systems for electronically transferring money, has made certain banking services obsolete. High inflation and corresponding high interest rates have caused the elimination of many state and federal laws and regulations which pertain to usury limits and which appear to be counterproductive to the natural financial laws of supply and demand. There has also been a concomitant effort to deregulate many industries. This background paper briefly reviews the changes occurring in one segment of the financial services arena--interstate banking.

Bank Holding Company: A parent company which controls one or more subsidiary banks. Generally the subsidiary banks, to avoid being classified as branches, must operate under separate charters, in which case each has its own capital base, separate banking facility and its own employees. Branch Banking: A system of banking whereby a single bank has separate offices in different geographical areas. Full or restricted intrastate branch banking is permitted in more than three-fourths of the states.

Interstate Banking: Branch banking or group banking that occurs across state lines. Currently, "interstate branch banking" is illegal under federal law. Intrastate Banking: Branch banking or group banking that occurs within a single state.

Overview of the Current Banking System

There are approximately fourteen thousand separate bank operations in the United States. This is, in part, an effect of the dual system of regulation. This figure compares to only eleven banks in Canada, a country with a national system of regulation. While a large number of banks in the United States might indicate active competition, which is not necessarily the case.

Interstate Banking was the regulation written to prevent banks from doing business across state lines or at least keep it under control. As we all know, that was changed a number of years ago, and the results have turned out to be what we have experienced a few years ago. The "too big to fail" concept fell on its butt, and the government and monopolies looked for someone to blame it on.

Before the financial crisis came to full force in 2008, shifts in the industry and society set the stage for temptation.

The 1999 repeal of the Glass-Steagall Act broke down the walls between retail and investment banking, allowing banks that take consumers' deposits to also engage in risky Wall Street-style gambles. At the same time, the government was aggressively promoting home ownership. And in 2004, regulators bowed to industry pressure to loosen rules about the reserves that investment banks had to hold, allowing them to take on more risk.

In response, bankers issued mortgages to people who couldn't prove their income, making more money as they made more loans. The banks repackaged home loans into investment products and sold them off to pension funds and other investors, giving them less incentive to worry about whether the loans were good or bad.

The banking industry became a big profit center in itself, not just a tool for moving money through the economy. The rewards got too big, too fast and too seductive, many industry insiders agree.

The banks' compensation structures made it difficult for employees to speak up if they saw anything that made them uneasy, current and former bankers said.

Bonuses were rewarded partly on team performance, so people were disinclined to object to questionable practices. Banks emphasized teamwork to the extreme, so people who spoke up could be seen as disloyal. The units that churned out the most revenue held the most sway with executives and other decision makers.

CHAPTER 8

THE TRUTH

Can we get the TRUTH with all the conflicting
diagnoses from the elected so called experts?

A recent article asks where are the fifteen million jobs that were supposed to have been created or saved in the last ten years. Someone other than the government and the media designated experts need to tell us honestly what they think a *"saved job"* is.

That is ***double-talk for a job that is a delayed termination or layoff.*** The essence of this article is that if we don't educate the generations to come, we won't have any jobs for them.

What about the ones needing jobs right now? The number is not 9.8 percent; we think it is closer to 25 percent. We are sure someone will say prove that the unemployment is that high.

Thomas Jefferson:

The democracy will cease to exist when you take away from those who are willing to work and give to those who would not.

Could this be a message to the chronic unemployed or Entitled Generation?

There was mentioned in an earlier article that incumbent politicians know 6 months before the election if they are going to win or not. If you look closely you will see how much the voting districts have been changed so the constituency supports the candidate's party.

There articles being written about the large amount of money sitting on the sidelines that is not being invested because of all of the uncertainty. Some of the business writers have estimated it to be 2 trillion dollars.

What a bunch of wimps. You give the small business a level playing field and 10% of that money and we will have full employment in 2-5 years.

All the while our governments on all levels are doing what they can to make it harder for new business startup or business expansion in order to make it look like they have a reason to have a job.

> Loyalty to the country always. Loyalty to the government when it deserves it.
>
> Mark Twain

The excerpts below come from an article that quotes federal officials. It is interesting that the authors say the labor market will not normalize for four to five years.

At the pace of improvement projected by Fed officials, "**it could take <u>four to five more years</u> for the job market to normalize fully**," Fed Chairman Ben S. Bernanke said Jan. 7 in testimony to the Senate Budget Committee after the jobs report. The workforce, those with jobs or looking for work, shrank by 260,000 workers last month, sending the share of the population in the labor force down to a 26-year low of 64.3 percent, the Labor Department's national report showed Jan. 7.

Unemployment stuck above 9 percent is one reason why President Barack Obama last month signed an $858 billion bill extending all unemployment benefits.

This article was in Bloomberg on 1/26/2011.

If you read that closer, the author seems to be saying that the state figures are subject to larger errors. The Federal Reserve System is taking a survey for the same information but claims it is more accurate than the states' information. These are the same people who can't predict a budget and live within it for an hour. The Federal Reserve System that is in charge of the banks and has supposed to be keeping them under control has failed miserably and can't count accurately. The banks who will fine you for not keeping your account balanced can't keep theirs balanced. What they continue to admit without coming right out and say it is that they don't know what is going on or how to fix it.

Because We Can't Handle The Truth!!!

Here is an article also delivered by the Federal Reserve System. We are going to have to release this book soon, because these articles prove our point over and over. They continue to contradict themselves.

In his first regular news conference, Federal Reserve Chairman Ben Bernanke said the central bank was continuing its stimulus policy_because it was projecting slower growth in the economy with only a modest uptick in inflation. The Fed cut its growth estimate for 2011 to between 3.1 percent and 3.3 percent from a January forecast of 3.4 percent to 3.9 percent.

It is another example of the numbers changing. It comes every few days.

RUSH: By the way, do you remember that big, big report, economic growth, fourth quarter of last year, and 3.2%, remember that? What did we tell you? We told you to hang on, sit tight, and be patient for the revised number. It won't be that good. And it wasn't. "The U.S. economy grew at a 2.8 percent annual rate in the fourth quarter, slower than previously calculated and less than forecast as state and local governments made deeper cuts in spending." Once again, economic growth revised downward, not 3.2%, but rather 2.8% in the fourth quarter.

UNEMPLOYMENT DROPS TO 8.9 PERCENT, NEARLY TWO-YEAR LOW; EMPLOYERS ADD 192K JOBS

In this March 1, 2011 photo, Mariam Bario, recently relocated to Seattle from Kenya, fills out an application with others at a job fair, in SeaTac, Wash. Employers in February hired at the fastest pace in almost a year and the unemployment rate fell to 8.9 percent _ a nearly two-year low. (AP Photo/Elaine Thompson)

Jeannine Aversa, AP Economics Writer, On Friday March 4, 2011

WASHINGTON (AP) -- Employers hired in February at the fastest pace in almost a year, and the unemployment rate fell to 8.9 percent -- a nearly two-year low.

The economy added a net 192,000 jobs. Factories, professional and business services, education and health care were among the sectors that hired. Retailers, though, trimmed jobs. State and local governments, squeezed by budget gaps, slashed 30,000 jobs, the most since November. Federal government hiring was flat.

In Feb 2012 it was reported that unemployment dropped to 8.3%. if you read the articles above you get the idea that this may not be true either. Could it be an election year????

Every time you turn around, the unemployment numbers are being changed and rarely if ever for the better.

Recently they got excited again because the employment numbers went back up but they did not want to tell everyone that they were the seasonal part time hiring for the Holidays.

In the following articles, the Federal Reserve System did not tell the American People about the money lent overseas while allowing foreclosure and bankruptcies caused by incompetence and excess.

In article after article, the American People see contradicting numbers concerning the health of the economy. It would be like going to the doctor and getting 10 different blood pressure readings at the same visit.

In the information age, and the speed of that information, why are the American People not getting the truth? We will summarize: government is lying to us.

The American People have been fed so much conflicting information that we reached the point that we don't have a clue what to believe.

They really don't want the American People to know the truth because they know we would throw all of them out. If the American People had a nickel for every time someone said that that the economy had turned the corner and then in the next paragraph said that the improvement will take five years, we could probably pay off the national debt.

The reports of how the economy is doing and what our confidence level is go back and forth. Small Business can and will turn this around but not with the current congress in office. Congress seems to believe that the large companies, car companies, or government are going to employ enough to lower the rate. It's not going to happen. It is impossible for the large companies.

This is like the same line they have been feeding everyone that taxing the rich more will balance the budget.

That is just not the truth and no one can prove those numbers either.

The American People have to know that we are getting the truth on a daily basis rather than slanted propaganda. We know good news doesn't sell papers or make the twenty-four-hour news cycle, nor does it serve government and Media's purpose of keeping the voting public stirred up against each other. I guess it would be boring to hear the truth. The American People can handle it; we have proven we can handle things that would have permanently crippled other countries. Americans always come through in these situations.

The following report concerns us greatly about our government's real concern for all of our health.

The American People cannot trust the numbers, and this next story should give you chills as to why we cannot trust a lot of other things in Washington, DC. Some would call this partisan we call this plan stupid that our government would act this way. What is the motivation?

What if I told you that the chairman and CEO of IBM, Samuel J. Palmisano, approached President Obama and members of his, before the healthcare bill debates, with a plan that would reduce health-care expenditures by nine hundred billion? Given the Obama administration's adamancy that the United States had to make health care (read: health insurance) affordable for even the most dedicated welfare recipient, one would think he would have leaned forward in his chair, cupped his ear, and said, "Tell me more!"

What if I told you that the cost to the federal government for this program was zero? What if I told you that, after two meetings, instead of embracing a program that was proven to save money—a private-sector program costing the taxpayers nothing and that was projected to save almost one trillion dollars—*President Obama and his team said, "Thanks, but no thanks" and then passed one of the most despised pieces of legislation in U.S. history? It's all true.*

Palmisano, the Chairman of the Board and CEO for IBM, said in a recent interview with *The Wall Street Journal* that he offered to provide the Obama Administration with a program that would curb healthcare claims fraud and abuse by almost one trillion dollars but the Obama White House turned the offer down.

Mr. Palmisano is quoted as saying during a taping of The Wall Street Journal's Viewpoints program on September 14, 2010: "We could have improved the quality and reduced the cost of the healthcare system by $900 billion...I said we would do it for free to prove that it works. They turned us down."

A second meeting between Mr. Palmisano and the Obama Administration took place two weeks later, with no change in the Obama Administration's stance. A call placed to IBM on October 8, 2010, by FOX News confirmed, via a spokesperson, that Mr. Palmisano stands by his statement.

Speaking with FOX News' Stuart Varney, Mort Zuckerman, Editor-in-Chief of US News & World Report, said, "It's a little bit puzzling because I think there is a huge amount of both fraud and inefficiency that American business is a lot more comfortable with and more effective in trying to reduce. And this is certainly true because the IBM people have studied this very carefully. When Palmisano went to the White House and made that proposal, it was based upon a lot of work and it was not accepted. It's really puzzling...These are very, very responsible people and don't have a political ax to grind.

In Mr. Obama's shunning of a private sector program that would have saved our country almost $1 trillion in healthcare expenditures, presented to him as he declared a "crisis in healthcare," he proves two things beyond any doubt: that he is anti-Capitalist and anti-private sector in nature and that he can no longer be trusted to tell the truth in both his political declarations or espoused goals.

We said earlier that no matter what you told some people, they would not believe it. The credentials of the CEO of IBM and lack of a political axe to grind continue to prove that the government's agenda is something else.

If the government had taken the money that was passed and spent on the stimulus bill ,what they said no to with IBM and what they have paid out in unemployment over the last couple of years and loaned it to the 5.8 million small businesses they would have full employment and on their way to a balanced budget.

CHAPTER 9

THE FUTURE OF
SMALL BUSINESSES

The future of small business is at a crossroads. It will be diffi-cult trying to pick the right track to a healthy future with all the conflicting information and obstacles placed in the way.

Now that the Internet has become such a standard of life, we see more and more home businesses. If this trend continues, you will see the type of small business that does little hiring.

Compare the number of employees per million dol-lars of revenue for Internet-based companies versus other industries with similar revenues. If you are not watching the buyouts and mergers in these businesses, you are miss-ing how big these companies are becoming. Their buyouts of the new web based companies are increasing the unem-ployment numbers.

Wall Street analysts have started to draw attention to companies that come into the "150 employees and above" cat-egory of small business. They call them *gazelles* because of the numbers they are hiring and how quickly they are growing.

These small businesses will want to be careful, because the minute Wall Street sees these companies on the radar, they will either buy them (which is not necessarily bad for them) or the large corporations will start providing the same service or products and stop their growth. When they buy them, they absorb the business and use probably less than 20 percent of the total employee count, if that, in their infrastructure. This situation happens time and time again. These companies are not being replaced.

Lawyers are on our list of groups who are causing the dif-ficulty for small business startups and survival. If you come up with a business idea or a patent, and someone wants to steal it, it comes down to how much money and time you have to defend it. Small businesses generally do not have either. Normally the companies stealing are the Large ones who have the large check books and Small Business cannot compete with that. The case is usually settled, and the only people who make money are the lawyers. This just allows the deadly virus to spread.

Vision and patience are lacking when all parties are looking for the big score. *This is why people, institutions, and the government are not looking to small businesses to pull us out of the current economic crisis.* They talk a good game but their actions do not live up to the rhetoric. The days of instant gratification and the quick fix are upon us.

Many business writers try to tell us that the big-box stores, the chains, the manufactures (with modernization and automation), and mega-companies will make up for the loss of growth in small business hiring. Every time the chain stores and manufacturers grow and get more auto-mated, they cut more jobs than they hire through growth. They cannot and will not make up for the hiring of the small businesses that they are putting out of business.

If you have a problem believing that automation enabled by the evolvement of computers is costing jobs then listen to this. One of the largest Home Improvement Companies has a distribution center in the south. This center is so computerized that when an employee at the store records on a handheld device that they need prod-ucts. The product is delivered to the distribution center and goes through the center and is never warehoused. The total time that it is in the building is 25 minutes.

Just 5 years ago the same process would have taken 10 times the labor and weeks in time. That is progress but at the cost of jobs.

This is why the government is trying to hire more to hide the fact that companies are not,(guess who contributes the most to all parties) and will not be doing it for quite a while, but doing so is costing us more and more in taxes. Without jobs, who can afford to pay the taxes?

There have been examples of Internet companies that buy property in depressed economic areas and build buildings close to a million square feet to house the equipment. They have unlimited resources and will pick a community that needs the jobs and will leverage great tax incentives. They then transfer in the workers needed to run their business and in truth it does nothing for the community at all

This is what is going on with the new economy, and when you have so many unemployed people who were trained in the service, construction, or manufacturing sector, they are not going to be the wave of future employment.

THE CURRENT SUPPLY OF WORKERS—

THE POTENTIAL VACCINE FOR PREVENTION OF STAGE 4 OR THE ACCELERATION TO A QUICKER MORE PAINFUL DEATH.

THE SELF ENTITLED GENERATIONS EFFECT ON THE DISEASE.

When the banks lend and the other groups mentioned get out of the way, we have a difficult issue as to who is going to pull us out of this economic sickness.

This is the time for new business start-ups and for business expansion, but the economic environment is not healthy. Everyone is focused on something that has nothing to do with the long-term health of our economy.

The following article gives you an indication of what a lot of the current supply of unemployed workers has to do.

Fidelity reported that, as of the second quarter, 2.2% of all 401(k) participants had made a *hardship withdrawal* at some point over the preceding 12 months. That's up from 2% in the prior year, and was the highest level in 10 years. At the same time, the percentage of 401(k) participants that had an outstanding loan from their account rose to a record high of 22% in the second quarter. The average loan amount was $8,650 at the end of the quarter. Boston-based Fidelity has $844 billion in retirement assets under management.

The top reasons people took loans and made withdrawals were to prevent foreclosure or eviction, pay for college, or purchase a home, according to the firm. *"The current economy has forced some workers to borrow from their 401(k) accounts in order to pay for critical living expenses, ultimately jeopardizing their future retirement*," said James MacDonald, president of workplace investing for Fidelity Investments. He added that for some investors "taking a loan or a hardship withdrawal from their 401(k) may be their only option because it's their only form of savings. However, we want to make sure that before workers tap their retirement accounts prematurely, they are fully educated about both the penalty that may be incurred and the long-term implications for their retirement." By Aaron Smith, CNNMoney.com staff writer August 20, 2010: 4:33 PM ET

In many cases, the older workers bring a great diversity of skills to the table and need to have jobs that utilize their skills.

This younger self entitled generation that is coming in behind the baby boomers seem to want something to be given to them because they were raised to believe that they did not have to work for it. This creates a dilemma of a different type. This unfortunately brings back the breeding ground for the unions. The unions in the past had a place when the workers were being abused. Over the past 30 years or so they have been a haven for protecting workers from having to work like the rest of us. This self-entitled group will be looking for someone to take care of them because they have no clue about work ethic.

Could this be the same group protesting and camping out on Wall Street and other Cities?

Long term employment will not be solved by sticking people at a register and making them beg for more hours at minimum wage.

There is something to be said for all work if you need to put food on the table, so to speak.

Watering down or disrupting the delivery of the Medicine (Employees).

McDonald's is having something they're calling "national hiring day." "McDonald's will hold its first national hiring day at its restaurants and via its website on April 19 to fill the openings at its restaurants across the US." They want to fill 50,000 jobs on that day. Now, that's cool. That's fine. No problems here at the EIB Network. But do you remember, let's go back to the 1980s, or any recovery, any economic recovery presided over by a Republican president. I'm sure you'll all remember the left and the Democrat Party deriding so many of the new jobs being created as worthless hamburger-flipper jobs, remember? Even during the eighties, during Reagan, during Bush, whenever there was an economic recovery, the Democrats, "Yeah, but they're worthless hamburger-flipper jobs." Now celebration, McDonald's wants to hire 50,000 people, fill 50,000 jobs on April 19.

The media is ecstatic. The Democratic Party talks about what a great impetus for the economic recovery Obama is, yet mention nothing here deriding the *kinds* of jobs. Nothing here about them being hamburger-flipper jobs. It's just interesting. Remember, folks, we have the facts on our side. The Democrats, however, own the narrative. Our never-ending battle is always going to be with the media.

Dialogue from the Rush Limbaugh Show

The truth is that they did not come anywhere close to hiring 50,000 workers.

MCDONALD'S TO SHAKE UP FOOD ORDERING SYSTEM

By Louise Lucas in London

Published: May 15 2011

McDonald's is to change the way customers order its meals in Europe, partly replacing cashiers and the use of banknotes at its 7,000 fast-food restaurants in the region with touchscreen terminals and swipe cards.

"Ordering food has not changed for 30 or 40 years," said Steve Easterbrook, president of McDonald's Europe, in an interview with the Financial Times.

The move is part of the fast-food chain's efforts to woo cash-strapped customers by making its restaurants more convenient and convivial. It is refurbishing stores, and introducing longer opening hours and new menus.

At a time when many retail and consumer companies are racking up sluggish or even shrinking sales in Europe, McDonald's like-for-like sales rose 5.7 per cent year-on-year in the first quarter – the highest growth out of its three main geographic regions.

Mr. Easterbrook said that the changes would make life easier for consumers as well as improve efficiency, with average transactions three to four seconds shorter for each customer. McDonald's European stores serve 2m customers a day.

If you use their math and numbers, this will reduce their staff at these 7,000 sites by at least 24,000 employees.

Weiky Filho, a student enjoying a burger at McDonald's in Wimbledon, London, was in favor of the changes. "You don't need to communicate with staff and it would be much quicker," he said.

But Joe Surkitz, 21, was less convinced. "I'm looking for work and if there's more machines doing jobs I'll find it harder. Plus you won't get service with a smile."

Mr. Easterbrook said that the new technology would allow McDonald's to harness more information about customers' ordering habits. Supermarkets and other retailers have huge databases of information on customers' shopping habits, which they gather from loyalty cards.

Diners at the 1,200 McDonald's outlets in the UK will shortly be able to pay by simply swiping a Visa debit card, just as London's commuters can swipe their Oyster cards at train stations.

Less than 1 month later they are showing what a mega company with the money to afford the automation will put into play. The act of putting in these self-help terminals will have a devastating effect on employment levels at this company. So we see that instead of not only missing the mark of hiring 50,000 by ½ that they could wind up through this automation costing more than 200,000 their jobs throughout the system.

We are not sure individuals ordering for themselves will help with one of the biggest health problems out there. (Obesity)

The American Employee had better wake up fast and realize that there is no free ride because our Government currently is the sickest entity of all.

Enough of our Testament! We have given more than enough reasons for how we plan dividing up our estate and how sick we are now. We need to let you know what we plan to leave to the parties responsible for the illness of small business and therefore the economy.

CHAPTER 10

WE BEQUEATH THE FOLLOWING

We felt it important to let Americans know what we will be leaving in our <u>Will</u> and to whom.

Remember our disclaimer before, that there are people in all of these industries that are exempt from the ones that mess it up for everyone else.

BANKS

We bequeath you Barney Frank and Chris Dodd.

"Whoever controls the volume of money in any country is absolute master of all industry and commerce."

James Abram Garfield

Abraham Lincoln said:
"I have two great enemies, the southern army in front of me and the financial institutions, in the rear. Of the two, the one in the rear is the greatest enemy.....

Someone obviously bequeathed you or made you feel empowered to do the following:
- The ability to be bailed out with our money All the while, when things are tough, you are raising your rates and fees.

- The ability to take back the homes of people knowing full well that you should not have loaned the money in the first place The opportunity to disguise the fact that you are trying to work with these people when you have found a way to make money off the foreclosed houses.
- How to change from a few years ago throwing money at all consumers and then doing nothing but sitting on the same customers money like an old hen.
- Changing the basics for making a loan from the Three Cs: character, collateral, and capacity. It has become collateral only.
- You do not need to get to know the person or company borrowing money. This has resulted in no personal service.
- You're not admitting it, but you have a formula that you work from, and there is no fluctuation from it.
- That you really don't need managers any longer. We could fill the loan form online or at an ATM, and a computer could tell us "no" just as easy.
- That you have made the rules that if the borrower owes the less than million dollars, they are a debtor and a liability, and if the borrower owes you fifty million, they are a partner.
- That for some reason you will destroy a small business in a minute but will do everything to work it out with the larger debtors.

INSURANCE COMPANIES

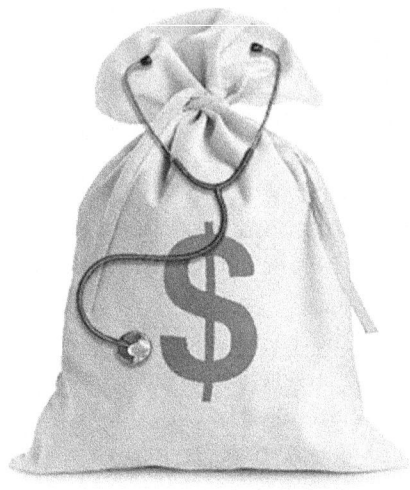

'We know how to punish retailers and manufacturers that don't provide quality and value. But we're lousy at fighting effectively for what we really need -- reliable insurance policies; affordable health care; safe, healthy food."

-- Shoshana Zuboff, writing in Fast Company magazine

For almost seventy years the life insurance industry has been a smug sacred cow feeding the public a steady line of sacred bull.
Ralph Nader

WE BEQUEATH THAT YOU PROVIDE FLAT RATES FOR ALL AGES AND NO PREEXISTING CONDITIONS AS WELL AS:

- A conscious. Lord knows you need to find one.
- To use the technology available today and cure almost all diseases including Cancer. DO IT.
- To correct the fact that you are one of the worst in this group when you make up the rules as you go and raise rates for any reason you decide. Your monthly costs are as much as house payments now. You really are one of the worst industries for the economy.
- The inability to make up the rules as you goes along. You used to cover test. Now you have decided not to and there are people who cannot afford an MRI and will die because of your greed.
- The integrity to see the how Bill Boards where the Doctors are all standing up in their nice starched white coats smiling and the ad reads "We are here to help you with your cancer is pathetic. This just proves that that you have lost your way.
- *The courage to take the Profit out of the business.*
- Not having the money to run these ads with lizards, women with too much make-up and people wrecking their cars trying to convince the public that they can save money when all you're doing is manipulating the deductibles.

Drug Companies

"If we doctors threw all our medicines into the sea, it would be that much better for our patients and that much worse for the fishes."

Supreme Court Justice Oliver Wendel Holmes, MD

We are happy to bequeath you the following:

Severe allergic reactions (rash; hives; itching; difficulty breathing; tightness in the chest; swelling of the mouth, face, lips, or tongue); bizarre behavior; black or bloody stools; chest pain; confusion; decreased concentration; decreased coordination; exaggerated reflexes; fainting; fast or irregular heartbeat; fever, chills, or sore throat; hallucinations; memory loss; new or worsening agitation, panic attacks, aggressiveness, impulsiveness, irritability, hostility, exaggerated feeling of well-being, restlessness, or inability to sit still; persistent or severe ringing in the ears; persistent, painful erection; red, swollen, blistered, or peeling skin; seizures; severe or persistent anxiety or trouble sleeping; severe or persistent headache or dizziness; significant weight loss; stomach pain; suicidal thoughts or attempts; tremor; unusual bruising or bleeding; unusual or severe mental or mood changes; unusual weakness; vision changes; worsening of depression.

For the great drugs that you have come up in the past that have done great things for our society we say thank you, for the excesses above that dominate the market, we refer you back to the side effects.

WALL STREET

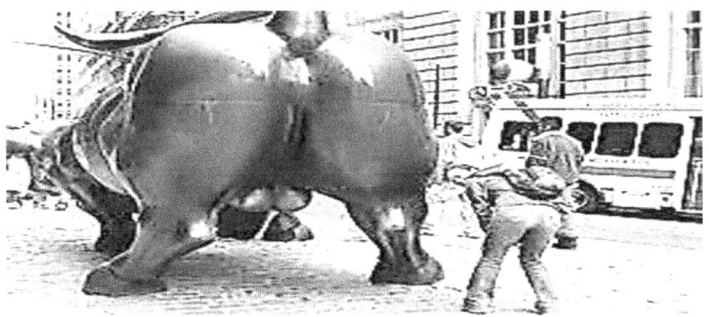

Why would we bequeath you greedy manipulative people anything?

We would like to bequeath you a conscious, but you sit and run the economy like the pit boss at a casino and the minute it starts taking off you help push it past reason and then when it draws back you do the same and all the while making money off of orchestrating it. Greed is such an ugly and addictive drug.

- We also bequeath you the same side effects to the ones left to the drug companies.
- No, we leave you one more thing. The current occupiers get to camp out on your front lawn and you have to feed them and let them in to use the bathroom.

LOBBYISTS

"It's time for Congress to go cold turkey and stop feeding at the lobbyist-funded trough"-- *Sen. Russ Feingold*

"Few men have virtue to withstand the highest bidder."
George Washington

WE DISOWNED YOU THE DAY WE KNEW WHAT YOU DID FOR A LIVING, AND WE SLAPPED ANYONE THAT MENTIONED YOUR NAMES IN PUBLIC.

- We bequeath that when you lie or attempt to do something that will harm any of the American People you will be stunned by a Taser until you quit and go find a good job.
- The only problem with that is someone from Congress would wait for you to stop having convulsions and take the money anyway.

LEGAL PROFESSION

John Adams, in the play "1776" said, I have come to the conclusion that one useless man is called a disgrace, two men are called a law firm, and three or more become a Congress.

WE BEQUEATH YOU TORT REFORM.

- The people who write the laws are the same ones paid by the millisecond to defend or change them. This is a conflict of interest.
- They did not write this will. We could not afford it...

BIG-BOX AND CHAIN STORES

HERE IS WHAT WE BEQUEATH YOU.

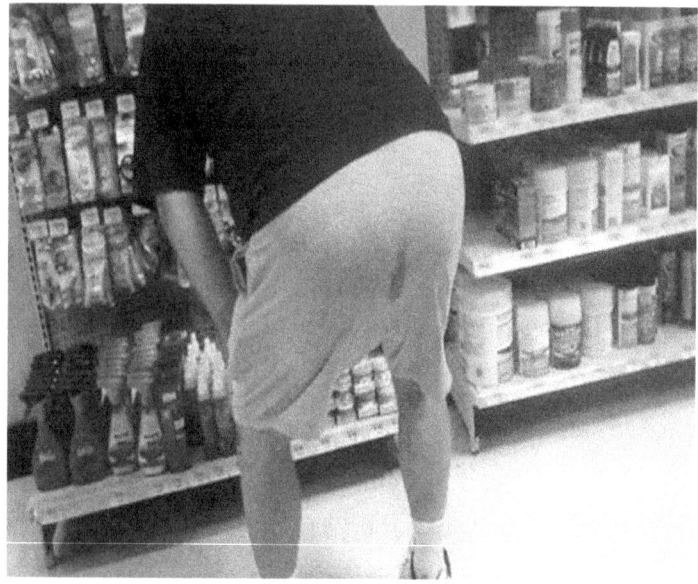

"The growing wealth acquired by them {corporations} never fails to be a source of abuses."--President James Madison

"Big business is not dangerous because it is big, but because its bigness is an unwholesome inflation created by privileges and exemptions which it ought not to enjoy."-- Woodrow Wilson, 1912

- Besides this we felt it important to bequeath you the ability to understand this sweet gift.
- You used to be one of us. You used to outsource to small business. You used to be loyal and remember

that you started as one of us. We don't look at you with envy or pride. We see you as a major part of what is destroying the economy and our way of life.

- You have reached the point that you don't care about the communities that you go into. If you cared at all, you would see the small businesses that you have destroyed. You have begun down a road of development that looks irreversible.
- Where does it end? It ends when the unemployment is so high and inflation increases so much that no one can afford your "everyday low prices!
- We bequeath you a piece of advice. Remember where you came from. Have the courage and vision to see where you current course as well as the economy is headed and do something to correct the course.

Also remember what Teddy Roosevelt said: In 1901, Roosevelt wrote Congress that the Constitution framers had not seen the startling rise and grave evils of corporate monopolies.

- You can't hire the number of Americans it will take to have full employment. At the wages you pay, they can't even afford to shop at your stores.

THE MEDIA

The man who reads nothing at all is better educated than the man who reads nothing, but newspapers.

Thomas Jefferson

Journalists are like dogs, whenever anything moves they begin to bark.

Arthur Schopenhauer (1788-1860) German philosopher.

WE BEQUEATH YOU:

Since we know you will not report the news truthful and balanced, we bequeath you a bad facelift, a membership in the Hair Club for Men and last but not least a raging case of uncontrollable diarrhea whenever the camera turns toward you. (That seems to be the only thing Hollywood can come up with that can get a laugh in a movie anymore).

- We bequeath you someone to dig up every ugly and embarrassing thing from your past and assassinate your character; we will do this in front of your family and the general public. You seem to enjoy doing this to anyone that enters politics you disagree with.
- We bequeath you a television that gets only 1 channel and that channel is of your competition 24 hours a day.

The following seems to be what you have tried to bequeath to us:

Your idea of creativity has grown to provide us with the following. You obviously started reality TV because of the lack of talented writers for quality shows.

How many times can you run a repeat of a show anyway?

We get to watch as so-called housewives from different cities have cat fights and just make outright fools of themselves. Maybe it is helping the plastic surgeons and fashion industries create jobs.

We get to watch while people eat laundry detergent, live in a home with 50 dogs, and others that want to show us how to kill hogs or make moonshine.

We get to watch people wreck their cars, bicycles, and skateboards.

We get to watch when a poor, tortured bull puts his horn up a person's butt.

We hope the tide may be turning on this incredible quality entertainment. The end of reality TV may be in sight. You are running out of subject matter.

May we so bold as to make some suggestions for future shows?

- How about TOP SHOT, Kidney Stone Wars.
- Dumpster Divers helping Hoarders.
- Septic tank adventures. What you can't smell you might see.
- Lifestyles of the dumb and dumber. Oh that's right, that's over half of all reality TV right now.
- And last but not least Politicians spending 3.5 million dollars a minute. Oh wait a minute that's not a reality show that's fact.

If any of these shows are already on or come out, we apologize for giving them the idea or potential plagiarism.

Government

For even more reasons that follow we bequeath our government the following:

Government is not the solution to our problem. Government is the problem. RONALD REAGAN, First Inaugural Address, January 20, 1981

"*In order to rally people, governments need enemies. They want us to be afraid, to hate, so we will rally behind them. And if they do not have a real enemy, they will invent one in order to mobilize us.*" *Thich Nhat Hanh*

- We bequeath you a great retirement, oh that's right you already gave yourself one.

Wages

Salary of retired US Presidents ....$450,000 FOR LIFE

Salary of House/Senate members ....$174,000 FOR LIFE
Salary of Speaker of the House ....$223,500 FOR LIFE
Salary of Majority/Minority Leaders .....$193,400 FOR LIFE

Average salary of a soldier DEPLOYED IN AFGHANISTAN - $38,000

Average income for seniors on SOCIAL SECURITY - $12,000

- *We also leave you this quote by Abraham Lincoln: Nearly all men can stand adversity, but if you want to test a man's character give him power.*
- We do this knowing that at some point, your day of reckoning is coming. We hope and pray that America will turn the current direction of government control back to the people.

- Almost 37 percent of the U.S. House of Representatives and 53 percent of the U.S. Senate are comprised of lawyers. It's like buying chicken wire from the fox.
- The examples and statistics in this book show how we have forgotten completely what the role of government is.

THE AMERICAN PEOPLE

We bequeath to you the following:

- The energy and motivation to get off the couch to register and go vote.
- Great shopping at boutiques in special places. (If you go there to ***price s***hop only, turn around and go back to the chains and big-box stores. The boutiques have to mark up prices to stay in business.)
- Diverse products, made in America.
- Nice restaurants with diverse menus and a casual, relaxed atmosphere.
- Your alternative is running through a drive thru while smelling the cars exhaust in front of you and the fast foods exhaust fans belching grease on your windshield and then driving down the road with your knees trying to control the steering wheel slamming a burger and fries down your gullet.
- Jobs with employers who know your name and family and care about your future.
- Businesses that know that they cannot grow without you and treat you well.

- Houses that were built by craftsmen. Instead of the track builders who were building a house in 90 days.
- The courage to take chances and start new business ventures.
- The love for this country and its Constitution that requires us to understand where we need to be going as well as where we have been..
- Taking the risks to provide for our families without being dependent on the government.

THE CORRECT MEDICINE TO CURE SMALL BUSINESS WILL ALSO CURE THE ECONOMY FOR THE UNITED STATES.

Before we start making these suggestions and after we have pointed out time and time again why we think the groups listed are the problem, here are the results from a respected International Survey firm that shows how its participants rated the groups mentioned in this book on TRUST.

- **Politicians in last place**

Over half of respondents expressed criticism of lawyers, bankers, trade unions, journalists, marketing specialists, managers, advertising experts and politicians.

As in previous years, politicians are bottom of the rankings and their approval rating has fallen by another 4% compared with the previous year, to stand at just 14%

In contrast, employees of financial institutions have fallen in the rankings, with just 57% of citizens claiming to have confidence in them in 2010. Since the beginning of the financial crisis in September 2008, bankers have seen a drop of 15 percentage points in terms of trust levels.

Firefighters enjoy the highest levels of trust internationally. The clergy and marketing specialists have suffered a considerable deterioration in their reputation, and trust in politicians has also fallen once again.

GFK Group.

HOW TO CORRECT THE
COURSE AND CURE THE
ECONOMY

EDUCATION

*America's future will be determined by the home and the
school. The child becomes largely what he is taught; hence
we must watch what we teach, and how we live.*

JANE ADDAMS

Franklin D. Roosevelt: *We cannot always build the
future for our youth, but we can build our youth for the
future.*

Our educational system of private and public schools and colleges is broken and must be changed. We are teaching students to take test and the SAT but not about how to make a living or create jobs. It needs to be turned upside down and redone.

If you look closely you will see that a lot of the college graduates are staying in school and getting Masters Degrees and more because they are smart enough to see that there are no jobs out there right now.

One of the greatest concerns right now is the constant increases in the cost for tuition. It will not be long before the only students able to afford to go to college will be the rich.

Have you noticed how well our special needs students are treated and taught? Guess what, we are all special needs students at one level or another, and we need to be taught in a way that allows us to reach our potential. (OK English teachers I know there have been run on sentences,etc. give me a break this is my first book)Some people catch on to math quickly while others can play an instrument. There are so many examples where the generalization of teaching is causing more problems than it is fixing. We have the technology and ability to determine what the needs are for a long time.

An article in *Time*, September 2010, was about public schools. If we read it correctly through the haze of political rhetoric, it says that we are now able to test children to find out what is working or not. The truth is if we treat each student as special, meet their needs, and help them be the best they can be then we will succeed.

Our educational system is the place to start educating and nurturing the next generation of entrepreneurs. It is not necessary to have people with master's degrees or doctorates to teach, and they need not wait until college to start. Teaching the fundamentals of entrepreneurship can be taught by retired small business owners. The byproduct of teaching this is that it would include the fundamentals of many of the subjects that are being taught in schools currently.

The school leadership and school boards don't have the courage to stand up for the students because of the problems generated by the decisions of the past. They are running a business with no accountability. There are exceptions, there are still some great teachers and administrators, but they are burning out fast.

Look at what has been going on in Wisconsin with the new governor. The state is going bankrupt, and he is trying to turn it around. The unions and the teachers would rather make the kids and the state suffer than work for a positive outcome for all. We guess we get to see what the unions have done for us.

There are many key subjects that need to be taught, and they include history, art, and math

Here are some of the cures.
- Treat all students as special-needs students.
- Test them early and often to help them find out where their gift and talents lie. Nurture them in that direction.
- Quit labeling them something like ADD or learning disabled. There truly are some that are but

gaining more grant money for doing this is almost criminal. Kids have enough pressure on them during this time they don't need to be saddled with something else.

- Prepare people for making a living or contributing to society in one fashion or the other.
- Go to year-around school years. Sorry teachers, the rest of us have to work year round, so you should to.
- Community colleges are doing more and becoming more popular as a way for people of all ages to get the skills they need to get jobs. They have become incubators for small business but are caught with too few resources. The departments and staff needed to have any kind of real impact are not in place. They need real-time small business people leading the departments and teaching in the classrooms.

Government

- Try telling the American people the truth. *We **can handle the truth.***
- Outsource at least 25 percent of all current government work to real small businesses after you cut the 30 percent of staff that are unnecessary and redundant. Protecting Government jobs and creating new government departments is not helping the economy or small business.
- Go to a flat tax or VAT only and help IRS employees find a job.
- Go to a line-item veto.
- Set term limits.

- Set a balanced budget based on the tax programs mentioned earlier, and keep it balanced.
- Outlaw lobbyists.
- Set tort reform.
- Protect small business through a complete revamping of the SBA. It would help to have no-interest loans for first three years and use a group of retired small business people to help incubate the ideas and startups of the new businesses.

Americans have generally admired the owners of small businesses and have desired the preservation of small enterprises, even at the expense of economic efficiency.

Nonetheless, governmental policies have often directly or indirectly furthered the development of big businesses in the United States. There has been a discrepancy between political rhetoric and reality, one that continues to the present day. *** Mansel G. Blackford History of Small Business in America

Our suggestions continue:

- Use the unused TARP, stimulus money, or proposed saved money on health care to help new small businesses get started. Your use of this money for other projects has been a complete failure.
- Level out the import/export side of things to keep more jobs at home. Tax imports in a way that levels the playing field. Make us energy independent. If

that means creating green jobs, good. All the jobs will be appreciated.

- Revise or revoke the laws or programs that you put into place that encourage large companies to merge and then outsource jobs and manufacturing overseas.

- Keep the military strong, and stay out front on technology, so no country will screw with us. We cannot and should not stick our nose in everyone else's business. If arms and weapons manufacturers need business that bad, let them lead the way in helping us become energy independent. Wars are not a way to stimulate the economy or take our minds off of it.

- Secure all the borders. Quit making this political. It should have nothing to do with gaining voters.

- If you look at history, we have supported both the right and wrong administrations overseas, and in all cases, it cost us more than we could afford. We have the CIA and the NSA; use the departments to the fullest potential. There are people out there who have ill intent against our country. Between those departments and the Military we have the ability to persuade their leaders that messing with the USA could be very dangerous. A Drone flying over their house every day would not be beneficial to their health.

- Plug the loop holes that allow the crazy amounts of money being raised and spent on political campaigns.

BANKS

Care enough about our economy to do the following:

- Go back to basics and become a part of the community again. Know your customers and allow the properly trained managers to make decisions instead of a bureaucrat from Washington.
- You got your start from making small business loans. Hire people that know something about small business and nurture them for success.
- Have the guts to tell the government to stay out of the banking business when it comes to things like CRA.
- Have a department in your company to outsource 25% of the work done for the bank to a small business in all of you communities instead of just the regional or national companies.
- Doing business with bigger is not helping the economy nor helping your bottom line. If it was, why are you losing so much money now and laying off so many people?
- Stop foreclosures on homeowners. Keep in mind that you are accomplices in creating this foreclosure nightmare in the first place and need to make up for your screw-up. ***You really can't believe that helping people to stay in their home is worse than letting it rot and then having it torn down after you have destroyed their lives.(or could you)***
- Quit the mergers. Small local banks are needed to help small business growth.

Insurance Companies

- Look for ways to assist small business start-ups.
- Give the start-ups lower rates that are not based on all the formulas and averages of other companies.
- Quit making up the rules for medical insurance coverage as you go along. Quit raising rates based on a whim.
- Give the customer service people that answer the phone a personality transplant.
- Give everyone the option when we call to Press 5, if we don't believe anything you are telling us.(We know that makes no sense but it makes us feel better)
- Take the profit out of the medical business and consider turning it into a performance based business where proactive health care and people being healthy reduces the rates is one of the goals.
- Quit making us pay rates based on everyone else's experience ratings.

Big-Box and Chain Stores

- Stop stomping on America's small business, stealing their business ideas, and sending jobs overseas.
- Bring those jobs back to the United States.
- Stop putting small specialty businesses out of business by buying their products and leveraging your purchasing power.
- Set aside a minimum of 20+ percent of all you need for suppliers and services for small businesses in the United States.

- Require and leverage you purchasing power with your vendors to have them do business with small business as well. This will prove that you care about this country and its employees. These are the people that shop in your stores.
- Quit trying to carry every product in the world that you know small businesses already carry.
- Leave small towns alone. They currently are the only fertile ground for new small business.

LOBBYISTS

- Take a hike. Find a real job. You are sucking the life out of the American dream.
- This country was not founded on buying off elected officials to make them puppets for a cause.
- Take the money in your accounts and donate it to cure cancer or other worthy causes.

The American Employee*For those feel that you need the government or a large company take care of you, it is time for a wake-up call.*

This article just proves that the private both small and large are not hiring. (0)

Christopher S. Rugaber, AP Economics Writer, On Friday September 2, 2011, 8:57 am

WASHINGTON (AP) -- Employers stopped adding jobs in August, an alarming setback for an economy that has struggled to grow and might be at risk of another recession.

It was the weakest jobs report since September 2010. The unemployment rate remained at 9.1 percent.

Your work ethic and loyalty will be the key to your success. Small business have tried for years to provide those opportunities and over the last fifteen years or so, we have found it hard to find workers who understood what it took to be a good employee. Maybe that came from a generation of parents who wanted to give their children more than they had and spoiled them. Maybe it came from the school system that pushed students through the system and did not prepare them to make a living.

No matter the reason, the country needs you, and you need jobs. You need to get over worrying or being jealous of the rich. Most of them worked to get there and unless you win the lottery you will not get what they have through taxes or crapping on their lawn. You will find that hard work will get and keep you a job. The other thing you will find is that you better get out and vote because that is what has gotten you in this predicament.

To all of the groups outlined in this book, we suggest that you read this next section carefully. Here are some lessons and thoughts learned from many years of experiences.

TO THE AMERICAN PEOPLE

- Small   Businesses of our age and experience qualifies us to give some advice.

- Small business believes some of our past leaders like Andrew Jackson and Teddy Roosevelt recognized the importance of protecting small businesses. They protected small businesses because they knew that we were what made this country great. We were what kept the economy on track, kept new jobs being created, and kept tax revenue coming in.

- You can see very clearly now that a lot of the Politicians in Washington have no clue what Small Business has done for this country and do not believe or care that it could pull us out of this hole that they have dug.

- When Congress has been influenced by the current political system to believe that "God Bless America" means "only after I have filled my pockets," you come to realize why we are in the shape we are in.

- The bottom line is that our government's finances are one giant Ponzi scheme. It has been for a long time and will be in the future unless something is done. If there were to be a true accounting of where the money was going we would be afraid of the actions by the public.

- Bernie Madoff actions were a misdemeanor compared to the stuff going on in government and many major corporations. These groups hide the true condition by refinancing it and packaging it in a more complicated way so that no one can figure it out.

- If the groups mentioned in this book will not correct the course with quick and decisive actions, we would like to suggest the following.
- We would like ask you to garner the anger, will power, and energy to do what it is going to take the stop this madness. We know you have heard some of these ideas in the past, but the good ones stick around.
- If you will support these ideas and get Washington, DC out of the way of small business, small business will get the economy back on track.
- Small business will create the kind of jobs that it will take to stabilize this economy and provide the type of income that will give you and your families the security that you have the right to work for. We have done this in the past without the need for fanfare.
- We have to be a key part of setting the agenda, keep it simple, stay the course, and expect results and accountability from all elected officials.
- The media is one the biggest obstacles. Somehow we need to send a message to the media. If everyone would just ignore or turn off the media for 6 months, we bet two things would happen: the world will still be around, and journalists will either have to change the way they report things, or they will be forced to doing infomercials only.
- There are other governments that vote in an entire philosophy and give the officials four years to implement their ideas. If the ideas work, the officials are kept, and if the ideas don't, the entire party

is thrown out. It isn't a one-party system, but it doesn't have two parties getting little done standing around complaining while we are the ones who suffer.

- We need more businessmen, not just politicians and lawyers. Negotiating with other governments is not about giving them our tax dollars for nothing in return.

- Find candidates that have the guts to tell like it is and that do not pander only to special interests. They are out there.

- Let's apply the Keep It Simple, Stupid (KISS) principle. The sooner Americans take, recognize good ideas, join together and get the common sense ideas that we have heard about and that are outlined in this book done, the sooner this will be behind us.

- Small businesses do not believe the only fields for future employment are healthcare or green energy. Nor do we believe that having the larger companies grow to be even larger is going to help and God help us if we depend on the government to get larger and hire.

- We better start raising our kids to know that not everyone that participates in anything deserves a trophy. And that they better pick a path for their education that will net them a job.

- Putting the right amount of money in New Small Business startups will generate more jobs than anything else than can be done. Look up the actual statistic of what the 700+Billion dollar stimulus netted in jobs. That money has gone for something else altogether.

- If you always do what you always did, you always get what you always got. That's Sothern for quit being an idiot.
- Americans are on our way to a mini revolution, but it needs to be a nonviolent one. If we don't take action soon, we have no one to blame but ourselves.
- Small businesses are not going away. We are not giving up. We may be old and sick, but we have faced odds like this in our past, and every time, we led the economy out of crisis. The difference was that our leadership had the courage and respect for our contributions to allow it to happen.
- They have called us small business for a long time. There are millions of us. That is not small.
- But we are Americans as well. If you use the statistics that there are 5.8 million small businesses with an average of 20 employees that puts us at 116,000,000 voters. That number makes us something to be reckoned with. Someone needs to start paying attention. This number could at the end of the day make the difference if someone gets elected or not.
- Last but not least BUY AMERICAN and BUY LOCAL and by all means seek out and buy from Small Business.

None of these ideas are new, but hopefully they have been shown in a way that brings them together for everyone to see what is going to heal Small Business and the economy.

In closing we mentioned earlier that small business has *26 billion days of on the job training*. If you want this economy to turn around you need to look no further than your local small business person and providing the right environment for new business startups. Support them, encourage them, buy from them and send the message clearly through your votes that you believe that they are the reason our Countries economy has been so strong in past.

If we allow the current direction we will have a permanent unemployment rate of 20% or more.

We also have to say that if all of the Large Companies at the beginning of the book remain the same size or get larger our ability to pay the bills will get tougher and tougher.

They along with the Government cannot hire all the people looking for work.

> 'Common sense is the knack of seeing things as they are, and doing things as they ought to be done."

> — Harriet Beecher Stowe

Small Business asks the America People, do we have the ability to do what needs to be done? The answer is yes.

This illness is not about choosing small business over the chain stores, it is about balance. Only the American people can control the direction of the future. We hope this book has enlightened and motivated enough people to help correct the current course.

God Bless America.

Visit us at http://www.thelastwillbook.com/

Go to our website and add your comments and click that you like the website to keep the movement going.

BIBLIOGRAPHY

Armor, John C., "Congress for Life: The Problem of Careerism in Congress and a Case For Term Limits," *InnerSelf*, http://innerself.com/content/index.php?option=com_content&view=article&id=5505:congress-for-life-the-problem-of-careerism-in-congress-and-a-case-for-term-limits&catid=154&Itemid=193

Aversa, Jeannine, "US Unemployment Drops to 8.9 per cent, Nearly Two-Year Low; Employers Add 192K Jobs," *The Associated Press*, March 4, 2011.

"Bernanke: Fed Sees Slower Growth, Uptick in Inflation," *CNBC*, April 27, 2011.

Beschloss, Michael R., *Presidential Courage: Brave Leaders and How They Changed America 1789-1989*, Simon and Schuster, 2007.

Conte, Christopher, "Small Business in U.S. History," *IIP Digital*, July 28, 2008.

Entenza, Rachel R., Maniam, Balasandrum, and Leavell, Hadley, "Is Wal-Mart Smothering Small Town America?" *The Entrepreneurial Executive* 10 (2005).

http://www.cruisesfun.com/largestcruiseship.shtml

http://www.leg.state.nv.us/Division/Research/Publications/Bkground/BP85-01.pdf

http://thevoiceofmarke.com/2011/01/ibm-offered-to-help-reduce-medicare-fraud-for-free/

Jeffrey, Terence P., "U.S. Tops $14.3 Trillion for First Time," *CNS News*, April 18, 2011.

Kavilanz, Parija, "Wal-Mart's Ready to Do Battle on Prices," *CNN Money*, April 11, 2011.

Kavilanz, Parija, "Wal-Mart: 'Our Shoppers are Running out of Money,'" *CNN Money*, April 28, 2011.

Keoun, Bradley and Torres, Craig, "Foreign Banks Tapped Fed's Secret Lifeline Most at Crisis Peak," *Bloomberg Report*, April 1, 2011.

Lanman, Scott, "Bernanke Sees Slow Drop in Unemployment Amid Recovery," *Bloomberg Report*, January 7, 2011.

Limbaugh, Rush, *The Rush Limbaugh Show*, April 4, 2011.

Moore, Stephen, "We've Become a Nation of Takers, Not Makers," *The Wall Street Journal*, April 1, 2011.

Pittman, Kirsten Valle, "New Program Aims to Help Lend Money," *Charlotte Observer*, September 28, 2011.

Radnofsky, Louise, "Big Payday or Some Hill Staffers," *Market Watch*, http://www.marketwatch.com/story/big-payday-for-some-hill-staffers-2011-03-06

Rexrode, Christina, "Bankers and Ethics: Is it Time to Talk?" *Charlotte Observer*, September 28, 2011.

Sechler, Bob, "GE Earnings Soar on Lending Arm," *The Wall Street Journal*, April 22, 2011.

Solomon, Deborah, "Small Business to Obama: Tax Cuts Won't Work," *The Wall Street Journal*, September 7, 2010.

Smith, Aaron, "401 (k) Withdrawals Spike," *CNN Money*, August 20, 2010.

Terlep, Sharon, "U.S. Hurries to Sell GM Stake," *The Wall Street Journal*, A

By Bob Ivry, Bradley Keoun and Phil Kuntz - Nov 27, 2011 7:01 PM ETMon Nov 28 00:01:00 GMT 2011

The Author has owned various small businesses for 30 years . He is an inventor with patents and trademarks in his name.

He has personally witnessed the destruction of the opportunities for small business by the entities mentioned in the book.

His hope for writing this book is to draw attention to the fact that Small Business has been and always will be the power of hiring in the economy and that stifling it is what creates crisis in the Economy each time.

www.ingramcontent.com/pod-product-compliance
Lightning Source LLC
Chambersburg PA
CBHW071429170526
45165CB00001B/451